THROUGH
CORRIDORS
of
LIGHT

for Monica

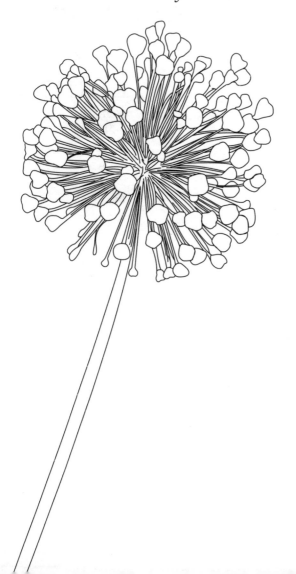

THROUGH
CORRIDORS
of
LIGHT

*Poems of Consolation
in Time of Illness*

EDITED BY
JOHN ANDREW DENNY

ASSISTED BY
SYLVIA SCOTT, ELIZABETH KERR &
MARGARET FOREY

Selection and editorial material copyright © 2011 John Andrew Denny
This edition copyright © 2011 Lion Hudson

The author asserts the moral right
to be identified as the author of this work

A Lion Book
an imprint of
Lion Hudson plc
Wilkinson House, Jordan Hill Road,
Oxford OX2 8DR, England
www.lionhudson.com
ISBN 978 0 7459 5547 6

Distributed by:
UK: Marston Book Services, PO Box 269, Abingdon, Oxon, OX14 4YN
USA: Trafalgar Square Publishing, 814 N. Franklin Street, Chicago, IL 60610
USA Christian Market: Kregel Publications, PO Box 2607, Grand Rapids, MI 49501

First edition 2011
10 9 8 7 6 5 4 3 2 1 0

Acknowledgements
The Acknowledgements starting on page 191 constitute an extension of this copyright page.

p. 155 Scripture quotation taken from The Holy bible, English Standard Version (ESV) copyright ©
2001 by Crossway, a publishing ministry of Good News Publishers. All right reserved.

All illustrations copyright © samposnick/iStock, unless otherwise stated.
p. 18 Yury Kuzmin/iStock
pp. 136–37 Helga Jaunegg/iStock
Decorative page rule pp. 13, 32 © Jamie Farrant/iStock

A catalogue record for this book is available
from the British Library

Typeset in 12/15 Arno Pro
Printed and bound in Great Britain by MPG Books

CONTENTS

§

Introduction 13

§

Part I: O Rose, Thou Art Sick

Part II: In a Dark Time, the Eye Begins to See

Part III: Cure Me with Quietness

Part IV: Look to This Day

Part V: Seasons of Beauty and Hope

Part VI: I Said to My Soul, Be Still

Part VII: Let Evening Come

§

$\mathscr{I}$NTRODUCTION

At times of intense emotion – when we are in love, are depressed, or have lost someone close to us – we naturally turn to poetry for its power to express what we can't find words to say, to speak the truth about what is happening to us, or for solidarity with others who have been through what we are now going through. Poetry helps us acknowledge and focus our feelings in strong, memorable language which comforts us and dignifies our emotions.

When we fall seriously ill, however, where can we find poetry to support us through this most difficult experience of our lives? Those with religious faith have an abundance of prayers and meditations on which they can depend at such times; readers, crossworders and knitters gain comfort from the distraction offered by their pastime. What is not widely known is that poetry, especially when relevant to the sufferer's predicament, can not only bring emotional and spiritual consolation but can also stimulate physical responses that are of immense therapeutic benefit. There is a clear need for a collection of such verse, which this book aims to fulfil.

The psychological effect of the onset of serious illness is in many ways like bereavement. It usually begins suddenly with the initial shock of diagnosis or realisation of illness, followed often by a collapse of morale, then denial, anger, bargaining, depression, and eventually – graciously or grudgingly – acceptance of the inevitable. People react to illness in very different ways, and illnesses themselves differ greatly in severity, duration, and their effect on individuals. What unites all of us who are ill is the deep sense of loss we feel – of precious faculties, of self-confidence, of something important in our relationships with others, of control over our future, perhaps even of our whole identity.

What we most need when we are ill is loving care, emotional support, and companionship. If we are lucky we will have a sympathetic partner, family or friends, though many of us today live alone, are socially isolated, or live too far away from those we love to be cared for by them. In hospital, care home or hospice there may be a chaplain or carer with whom we can share our anxieties and feelings of loss or isolation. If we are alone at home we may find a sensitive counsellor or therapist, or maybe someone from our local church, with whom we can talk through our feelings.

Whether or not we find such a person, it is almost impossible for anyone who has not been seriously ill themselves to understand fully the vulnerability and confusion an ill person can feel, and if we are left to manage alone, the feeling of neglect – irrational though it may be – can be deeply demoralising. Although we may cope well enough most of the time, in silent moments of the day or night when we have nothing to distract us from facing our diminished selves, we may dearly wish for a wise friend who understands what we are going through, who is calming, consoling, and able to give good advice about how we are to carry on with what may look like a very depressing future.

In compiling this book I have aimed to represent this wise friend by gathering the testimony of poets who have been through challenging times themselves, who can help us express our deepest feelings, inspire us to see our lives and our world in new and beautiful ways, and console us with comforting thoughts and images. To explain how I believe this can be of the greatest value to anyone who is ill, I will describe my own story and how I came to put together this anthology.

CABIN FEVER

The onset of my own illness was untypical in that it began not suddenly but imperceptibly at some time much earlier in my life, creeping up on me surreptitiously over several decades, slowly sapping my energy, stamina and mental clarity, until it finally brought me down with full-blown ME more than twenty years ago. (ME is a chronic neurological condition often conflated with Chronic Fatigue Syndrome.) When it struck I had no idea it was possible to feel so ill. The physical and mental exhaustion, confusion, nausea, pain, and noise and light intolerance were indescribable. My mind felt stunned. I could not read anything longer than a newspaper column, and even then I would forget the beginning by the time I reached the end. I was emotionally very fragile, often bored, and deeply depressed about my prospects.

My instinctive response to falling ill was to do what many people do – to behave as if nothing traumatic had happened, withdrawing into myself and avoiding opening up to my wife, family and friends. At that time I did not know how important it is for our wellbeing to be able to trust others and ask them for emotional support when we most need it. Although I usually had no problem asking for practical help, I found I could not share deeper feelings, especially those I felt awkward or ashamed about – feelings of helplessness, self-pity, grief for my old self, and a consequent frustration and even hostility towards many other people. By not recognising my need for help I made things far worse for myself than they might have been.

By great good luck, relief of a kind I could never have predicted came when a friend sent me a poem on a postcard – it was John Masefield's 'Sea-Fever' – which my wife blew up to A3 size and put on my bedroom wall. Until then I had spent most of my days lying on my back, gazing at the ceiling and half-listening to the radio. Now I was just as likely to be lying on my side, focusing my mind on a few lines of the poem. I was mesmerised by the music and the rhythm of its language, and I took comfort in saying its lines over and over like a mantra, which would run through my head at odd times of the day and night. To my delight I found that repeated reading set my imagination alight and briefly transported me out of my prison of boredom and frustration.

Before that time I had not been especially interested in poetry. Now I found that the more I read and reread Masefield's poem the more I absorbed and lived in it, until it almost became part of my own experience. Every few weeks I changed the poem for a new one, and those I found most satisfying had a gentle, musical quality that was soothing and mentally undemanding. I noticed how calm I became when reading of the coming summer in Matthew Arnold's lines: 'Soon will the high Midsummer pomps come on, / Soon will the musk carnations break and swell', which evoked the promise of June and reminded me of gardens I had known and loved; and when I followed W B Yeats's imaginary escape from the grey London streets to his 'Lake Isle of Innisfree', I felt the exhilaration of freedom from my own narrow London flat, which in reality I could rarely leave.

I was not surprised to learn years later that clinical studies of what happens when a person reads (or writes) poetry have demonstrated parallels with hypnosis, one of the tenets of which is that at an unconscious level the mind does not distinguish between real and imagined experience, even though consciously we know the difference perfectly well. Under hypnotic conditions a strongly imagined experience can reproduce the emotional effect of a real experience, as anyone who has been treated by hypnotherapy knows. Poetry can have the effect of slowing the reader's mind down to its alpha brainwave state of highest creativity, which it shares with dreaming. It also parallels hypnosis (and meditation) in the way it stimulates the body's production of endorphins – technically, opioid neuropeptides, which resemble opiates in their analgesic and euphoric effects. When my waking-dream state took me into Masefield's world of seafaring and comradeship, or Yeats's idyllic Innisfree, I found after several months that my feelings of being trapped began to dissolve as if I really had gone 'down to the seas again', and heard 'lake water lapping with low sounds by the shore'.

Sea-Fever
by John Masefield

I must go down to the seas again, to the lonely sea and the sky,
And all I ask is a tall ship and a star to steer her by,
And the wheel's kick and the wind's song and the white sail's shaking,
And a grey mist on the sea's face and a grey dawn breaking.

I must go down to the seas again, for the call of the running tide
Is a wild call and a clear call that may not be denied;
And all I ask is a windy day with the white clouds flying,
And the flung spray and the blown spume, and the sea-gulls crying.

I must go down to the seas again, to the vagrant gypsy life,
To the gull's way and the whale's way where the wind's like a whetted knife;
And all I ask is a merry yarn from a laughing fellow-rover,
And quiet sleep and a sweet dream when the long trick's over.[1]

---

[1] In seamen's jargon a trick is a stint at the helm.

THE MAN ON THE DESERT ISLAND

The longer one is ill, and the more isolated one becomes, the further one is liable to stray from emotional and social normality. I was beginning to feel like the essayist Charles Lamb's self-caricature 'The Convalescent': 'How sickness enlarges the dimensions of a man's self to himself!', he wrote, 'he is his own exclusive object.'

> Supreme selfishness is inculcated upon him as his only duty. He has nothing to think of but how to get well. He is for ever plotting how to do some good to himself; studying little stratagems and artificial alleviations. He lies pitying himself, honing and moaning to himself; he yearneth over himself; his bowels are even melted within him, to think what he suffers; he is not ashamed to weep over himself.

How deep I allowed myself to drift into this state I don't like to remember, only that it was for far too long. I already knew John Clare's poem 'I am; yet what I am none cares or knows', written when he was in a private mental asylum in the 1830s. In it he laments being caught in a 'living sea of waking dreams, / Where there is neither sense of life nor joys, / But the vast shipwreck of my life's esteems'. How I could sympathise when he complains that those he loves, 'e'en the dearest – that I loved the best – / Are strange – nay, rather stranger than the rest'. Illness turns you into an alien creature, making you as foreign to other people as they become to you.

As often happens when I browse through poetry anthologies, one poem in particular leapt out at me – this by Gerda Mayer – because it touched a nerve I was increasingly sensitive about:

The man on the desert island
Has forgotten the ways of people,
His stories are all of himself.
Day in, day out of time
He communes with himself and sends
Messages in green bottles:
Help me *they say* I am
Cast up and far from home.
Each day he goes to watch
The horizon for ships.
Nothing reaches his shore
Except corked green bottles.

The poem's message was inescapable. I had spent too long 'communing with myself', and I realised that as long as I lay back hoping someone would come and rescue me, life was passing me by. The poem was the trigger that decided me to start compiling this anthology. It was time for me to return to the world.

O ROSE, THOU ART SICK!

Poets have described writing poetry as a way of thinking about difficult and uncomfortable things, of taking fuller possession of the reality of their lives. The German poet and novelist Hermann Hesse was more explicit:

In its origin a poem is something completely unequivocal. It is a discharge, a call, a cry, a sigh, a gesture, a reaction by which the living soul seeks to defend itself from or to become aware of an emotion, an experience ... It speaks first of all simply to the poet himself, it is his cry, his scream, his dream, his smile, his whirling fists.

A poem written in a state of heightened emotion or crisis is a potent record of the poet's vision, and when communicated to the world can be a salve or even salvation for others undergoing similar experiences. It helps us make sense of things we can't quite articulate or even recognise. More than that, poetry differs from other forms of writing in that it is not just made up of words and thoughts but is a kind of incantation, a spell, intensified by the use of powerful language and animated and made memorable by cunning use of rhythm, alliteration, imagery, and other devices. A well-made poem sticks in the mind, where it stays to work its magic.

The poet John Keats believed that poetry should strike the reader as an expression of his or her own highest thoughts, almost as a memory of something already half known. Poems that spoke to me directly about my illness gave me words I desperately needed to express my feelings to myself, to release the pressure of silence, and to help me draw conclusions I had not yet registered. I wanted words that not only said everything I needed to say, but would bear repetition, and in repetition bring comfort even in their ominous message. When William Blake writes 'O Rose, thou art sick! / The invisible worm [my stealthy illness] ... / Has found out thy bed / Of crimson joy [my previous good health], / And his dark secret love / Does thy life destroy', he is leading me gently towards facing the possibility that I might never again be well. I realised that until I faced facts like this I could not hope to find peace.

An early discovery in my search for poetic self-expression was Po Chu-ï, a poet who suffered from an illness that sounded very like my own more than twelve centuries ago in Tang Dynasty China. An official in the emperor's palace, he fell ill at a time of personal crisis when both his mother and daughter died and his health collapsed. Not much is known about his illness except that it lasted for at least four years and caused extreme fatigue and digestive weakness. Two things kept him sane: writing poetry, even though what he wrote seemed to him 'slight and flavourless', and Buddhist meditation – 'If I had not learned "the art of sitting and forgetting", / How could I bear this utter loneliness?' He wrote several poems about the desolation of being ill for so long, far from his family, and living in poverty: 'Sad, sad – lean with long illness; / Monotonous, monotonous – days and nights pass …'; and later in the poem continues, 'The Four Seasons go on for ever and ever.' Po Chu-ï became my companion and my mentor. Suddenly I no longer felt alone. Here was a kindred spirit who had been through the same ordeal as mine many centuries ago, who was expressing in the most beautiful words the very feelings I now felt.

I too learned to meditate, to bring about in myself an elevated state of consciousness which suspended the pressure of time and distanced me from anxiety, stress, and undue concern about my future. I began with a rudimentary form called breath-counting, in which one slows and deepens the breathing, disciplining the mind to focus on a single changing number, and tuning in to a different level of awareness. When reading a poem after being in this relaxed state I found that it seemed to expand in my mind as it made more and more connections with my experience and imagination. It brought me to a new state of understanding which I can only describe as more grounded, more centred, more balanced.

THE HEALING ART OF
WRITING POETRY

To say that poetry can heal in any medical sense is only to exaggerate a known fact about its therapeutic effect. It is thought that the first recorded clinical use of poetry therapy was in the first century AD when the Roman physician Soranus prescribed verse tragedy for his manic patients and comedy for the depressed. In modern times in the US, Britain and increasingly throughout the world there has been a remarkable blossoming of the use of poetry-reading and -writing to bring about a healing state in patients in hospitals, care homes and even GPs' surgeries.

Emulating my mentor, Po Chu-i, I too began to write poetry about my life and illness, a process I found far more rewarding and revealing than anything I had previously attempted in prose. Writing poetry makes you concentrate your thoughts into their purest form and dig deep into your character, motivations and illusions. Poetry also requires you to express your feelings in imagery rather than try to describe them literally. Imagery, the language of the unconscious, can be understood on several levels. It bypasses the literal mind, revealing emotions and associations you were previously unaware of. Once out in the open, feelings of fear, guilt, hatred and despair lose their power to frighten or control. The act of writing poetry is both a prayer for help and an answer to that prayer, in that one begins to heal simply by putting one's feelings into words. One needs to hear or see certain things said so that they can be acknowledged and worked through.

Poetry can also take you in directions you could never have foreseen. Billy Collins, US Poet Laureate from 2001 to 2003, says that for him one of the pleasures of writing poetry is 'starting out not knowing where you're going and finding a way to get there. The poem becomes, not a whole expression of something you think or feel, but a journey through itself to an ending that is unforeseeable. In fact the ending is something that the poem is busy creating. It is almost as if the poem is the only way to access that particular ending.'

The poetry I wrote was not good, sadly, but that was not the point. It was the writing of it and the discoveries I made in the process that made it so worthwhile. If I started by feeling hopeless and at a loss as to how I should move forward, I would end by feeling encouraged and with a better understanding of myself. Nevertheless, the quality of a poem is so central to my enjoyment of it that I could never take much pleasure in my own work, and these experiments inevitably confirmed my original conviction that, for me, the most satisfactory kind of poetry therapy would involve working with what better poets had written during their own times of crisis and revelation.

POEMS OF CONSOLATION

Having discovered that the poems that had the most beneficial effect on me were those directly relevant to my situation, I began making a conscious effort to search for them, though I quickly found that they were not often to be found where they might have been expected. In previous centuries physical illness was not a popular poetic subject. In the Middle Ages illness and death were seen as resting in God's hands, to be accepted rather than bewailed, and it was not until the rise of individualism and the growth of introspection in the seventeenth century that so personal a concern as illness began to be even considered a possible subject for poetry.

The first poet I know of who devoted whole poems to physical illness was Anne Bradstreet (c1612-72), who, having emigrated in 1630 from the Midlands town of Northampton with her parents and husband to Massachusetts in the Puritan migration to America, bore eight children (two of whom died), suffered successively from smallpox, tuberculosis and paralysis, and lost her family home when it burned to the ground. Her poem 'Upon Some Distemper of Body' appears to be her first truly subjective verse describing details of her illness, although even while bemoaning her suffering she also thanks God for alleviating it:

> In anguish of my heart repleat with woes,
> And wasting pains, which best my body knows,
> In tossing slumbers on my wakeful bed,
> Bedrencht with tears that flow'd from mournful head
> Till nature had exhausted all her store,
> Then eyes lay dry, disabled to weep more;
> And looking up unto his Throne on high,
> Who sendeth help to those in misery,
> He chased away those clouds, and let me see
> My Anchor cast i' th' vale with safety.
> He eas'd my Soul of woe, my flesh of pain,
> And brought me to the shore from troubled Main.

Throughout the eighteenth and nineteenth centuries the poetry of illness was still a rarity, the prerogative of the eccentric, and only in the twentieth century, with the spread of psychoanalysis, did it enter the poetic mainstream.

When I began putting this book together I decided against making it an exhaustive anthology of 'illness verse', or simply a book of soothing poems; what I was interested in were poems that would help me and others cope with our conditions, that would give us words to express our feelings and transcend the limitations illness can impose on imagination. The poems I had gathered thus far were a random collection, ranging from straightforward accounts of poets' experiences of illness to something more like verse commonplace-book entries in my own Pilgrim's Progress through illness, registering different phases of need or interest and deepening levels of understanding. Most of them spoke in the persona of the poet, allowing me to experience them in the first person as expressions of my own self.

Often a poem would contain lines that encapsulated a truth I wanted to absorb, a motto to direct change in my life, or a mood I wanted to induce – for example, the anonymous 'Look to this day, / For it is life, the very life of life';[1] John Fletcher's 'Weep no more, nor sigh, nor groan, / Sorrow calls [brings back] no time that's gone'; or John Bunyan's 'Hobgoblin, nor foul Fiend, / Can daunt his Spirit: / He knows, he at the end, / Shall Life Inherit.'

Other poems were extended metaphors capable of various interpretations and associations. Tomas Tranströmer's 'Tracks', for example, blessed me with the most optimistic way possible of thinking about my illness, sparing me much anguish when I was stuck for months in the uncertainty of waiting for a diagnosis, and later when I learned that there is no cure for my illness. In this poem a

---

[1] 'Look to this day' has long been mistakenly attributed to the Classical Sanskrit poet Kalidasa, but according to scholars it is definitely not by him, nor by any other known Sanskrit poet.

train has stopped in the middle of a plain in the dead of night. All that can be seen outside are the moon (but few guiding stars) and some specks of light in the distance: 'As when someone has gone into an illness so deep / everything his days were becomes a few flickering points, a swarm, / cold and tiny at the horizon.' Like the stopping of the train, there was no apparent reason for my illness. Sooner or later either I would recover and continue on my way through life, or I would be forced to abandon my journey, get off the train and make my way to the nearest point of light. All I need do was be patient, and my predicament would resolve itself one way or another. The poem still helps support the patience and endurance I depend on and need to last indefinitely.

I also found it immensely consoling to read poets' thoughts on their own illnesses or injuries – such as Theodore Roethke's 'In a dark time, the eye begins to see / ... A man goes far to find out what he is', or Anna McKenzie's religious poem 'Starting Over', beginning 'And so we must begin to live again, / We of the damaged bodies / And assaulted minds' – or the philosophical advice by the former priest John O'Donohue 'For a Friend, on the Arrival of Illness', encouraging the friend to make of his adversity an opportunity for spiritual growth. Similarly, when sometimes morbidly dwelling on the (im)possibility of dying, I was grateful to the many poets who have written about their own approaching end – from Molly Holden's poems sensitively recording her decline due to multiple sclerosis, to John Donne's 'Thou hast made me, And shall thy worke decay?', John Keats's 'When I have fears that I may cease to be', and Christina Rossetti's 'Remember me when I am gone away'.

During my twenty years of illness my awareness of a dimension beyond myself has gone through many fluctuations, so that there have been periods when I have given no thought at all to my spiritual life, others when I wanted to explore my spirituality through meditation, and yet others when I became absorbed in my search for the God that 'is that great absence / In our lives, the empty silence / Within ...' (R S Thomas). Inevitably, the poems and prayers that supported me in these phases were characterised by their special poetic beauty.

An important part of coping with illness has to do with finding ways of cushioning the pain that constantly encroaches on every aspect of daily life, and many of the poems I was gathering answered this need – poems that evoked comforting images of nature, the passing seasons, friendship, music, sleep – so that simply reading them would transport me out of an often uncomfortable present into a peaceful, healing place in some normally unreachable part of my mind.

Frequent reading of certain poems – slowly and often out loud, a manner which can transform one's understanding of and openness to a poem – led me to learn many of them by heart (for the short time my mind would retain them), and when I did I found that they would acquire an extraordinary power that caused them to resonate more and more in my mind each time I spoke them, so that sometimes I was conscious of an almost transcendental response to the words. As the years passed, I felt a veil lift between me and an unsuspected dimension, and a change occur in the way I felt about my illness. By some subtle alchemy, my attitude to it changed from one of oppression to one of liberation and confidence in myself, bringing a degree of acceptance and contentment I had not previously experienced.

Another side-effect that demonstrated beyond doubt the analgesic effect of reading poetry was that when my pain was especially hard to endure, I could relieve it to a significant degree by immersing myself in poems that echoed my darkest and most painful feelings – emotional as well as physical – knowing that the effect would be intensely consoling. Furthermore, it is surmised that there is in our nervous system a sort of bottleneck known as a 'pain-gate' which limits the number of impulses that can pass from the body to receptors in the brain, so that we can significantly reduce our awareness of pain by giving our senses a surfeit of distracting messages to transmit. Anyone who has been ill for a long time knows how to diminish their suffering by using certain long-established methods of alleviating it – whether by practising yoga, meditation, dancing or other movement, multi-sensory stimulation, concentrating on an absorbing task, or engaging in an artistic – or poetic – activity.

THROUGH CORRIDORS OF LIGHT

My reasons for wanting to compile this anthology were partly self-serving – to draw out as many poems as could be found to help me with my own poetry-reading therapy (see 'An Invitation', below) – and partly to advocate the idea of such therapy for the benefit of everyone who is ill. First I needed to know whether there were many other people who used particular poems in the way I do – for consolation, support, encouragement, inspiration or escape. Following a series of letters and articles I wrote for general and support-group magazines describing the sort of 'Poems of Consolation' I was looking for, I received hundreds of suggestions and supporting comments. I was not surprised to find that the common characteristic of the majority of suggested poems was their euphony, their soothing musical quality, which was what set me on my quest in the first place and characterises most of the choices in this book. Nor was it a surprise to find that the most frequent suggestions were Yeats's 'The Lake Isle of Innisfree', the archetypal poem of escape from a dull or oppressive present to a paradise elsewhere, and Mary Oliver's 'Wild Geese', a poem of absolution (in this interpretation) for the guilt many people who are ill feel about not being able to fulfil their family or other responsibilities. Many correspondents sent poems that were inspirational or encouraging – W E Henley's 'Invictus' – 'I thank whatever gods may be / For my unconquerable soul', John Bunyan's 'Who would true Valour see', and Oscar Hammerstein's 'You'll Never Walk Alone' – while others spoke of poetry's calming effect, of its capacity to elevate their feelings, or of the way it 'sets your mind singing' when you read it.

Following a letter I wrote to *The Tablet* and an article for *The Church Times*, I received a large number of prayers, psalms and hymns, of which I include in this book some of the most poetic, since I believe they can speak just as much to non-believers as to believers. One correspondent quoted the playwright Samuel Beckett's view that 'all poetry is prayer', adding that 'all good prayers are usually also poetry', by virtue of using many of the same techniques, capturing an equally elusive intuition, and arriving at a similarly enhanced level of understanding.

My organisation of the poems into sections reflects the spiritual progression I have followed during the course of my illness (and I would guess many others have followed during the course of theirs). The titles of each part have been chosen as signposts on this path: *Part I: O Rose, Thou Art Sick* – helping to move beyond our initial fixation with pains and symptoms by confronting the pervasiveness of illness as part of being human; *Part II: In a Dark Time, the Eye Begins to See* –

starting to accept how great a change we must make in our attitudes if we are to find contentment; *Part III: Cure Me with Quietness* – learning to be still and to appreciate what we have; *Part IV: Look to This Day* – rebuilding courage and hope in the future; *Part V: Seasons of Beauty and Hope* – finding consolation in the cycle of the seasons; *Part VI: I Said to My Soul, Be Still* – addressing the spiritual dimension of our awareness of ourselves; and *Part VII: Let Evening Come* – meditating with the poets on the certainty of our death.

Whether such equanimity as I feel after more than twenty years of illness can be attributed purely to the consoling effects of the poetry I have gathered for this anthology, or whether it is partly also due to my practice of meditation – or a necessary combination of the two – I cannot be sure. However it may be, I send out this anthology in the hope that you will find in it as much comfort and inspiration as I and my fellow compilers have derived from putting it together, and I offer it to you in the same spirit as that in which the poet David Gascoyne ended his radio poem 'Night Thoughts':

Greetings to the solitary. Friends, fellow beings, you are not strangers to us. We are closer to one another than we realise. Let us remember one another at night, even though we do not know each others' names.

John Andrew Denny

AN INVITATION

In pursuit of one of my purposes in compiling this anthology – to draw out from other sufferers poems they find consoling in their illness – and suspecting that many readers may not find here the kind of poetry they perhaps expected to find, I invite you to send me your suggestions via a website I have set up with the title Poems of Consolation (poemsofconsolation.net), the best of which I hope will be included in a future edition of this book. I would ask that your suggestions arise from personal experience of illness, and that they be ones you yourself (or someone you care for) turn to for comfort or inspiration; that give you strength or courage; that change the way you feel about your illness; or that help you escape the bonds of your suffering or circumstances. If you do not use the internet and would prefer to contact me by post, please write care of the publisher of this book.

JAD

Follow, poet, follow right
To the bottom of the night,
With your unconstraining voice
Still persuade us to rejoice;

With the farming of a verse
Make a vineyard of the curse,
Sing of human unsuccess
In a rapture of distress;

In the deserts of the heart
Let the healing fountain start,
In the prison of his days
Teach the free man how to praise.

W H Auden

PART I

O ROSE, THOU ART SICK

William Blake
(1757-1827)

The Sick Rose

O Rose, thou art sick!
The invisible worm,
That flies in the night
In the howling storm,

Has found out thy bed
Of crimson joy,
And his dark secret love
Does thy life destroy.

Catie Jenkins
(*b* 1978)

Please Don't

Please don't tell me I look just fine,
Please don't say I'll be right in no time
When I can hardly make it through the day.
You don't have to live this life
So please don't tell me you know what it feels like
Or how it really is to be this way.

Please don't tell me I'm just a little tired,
Don't shake your head and say I'm not really trying
When I want to spend some quiet time in bed.
'Come on, let's get you out of the house,
We all have our ups and downs.'
You haven't heard a single word I've said.

Potions, pills and wonder cures –
I don't believe in miracles.
I only wish you understood the truth,
That to watch and wait and pray,
Live in hope from day to day,
Is all that either one of us can do.

Alison Tavendale
(*b* 1948)

Fraudulent

'You're a fraud,'
said my friend
as I showed her to the door.

And she was right:
the automatic smile,
the courteous
conditioned responses,
the self-denying need
to put others at ease
can only deceive.

And she was wrong
not to question or doubt,
not to care enough
to find out,
but happy to leave,
(comfort zone intact),
without having to believe.

As she climbs into her Suzuki,
she does not see me
collapsed on the bottom stair,
too sore to move,
too tired to think,
tears washing away
the Kabuki mask.

Sharon Brogan
(*b* 1948)

Fibromyalgia

I've become the princess I disdained as a child. I'll prove my
royal blood. Put twenty mattresses between me and that pea.
My bones will feel its sharp, hard curve, here, at the small
of my back. I am only sick, I am not dying, no faster

than I was before. I want to stretch my muscles across
the cool length of the blue pool. I want to walk four miles a day
in the rainforest, through the cedars, beneath the eagles and herons.
I want to laugh from the middle of my belly so hard my breasts

bounce. I want to throw Clancy's ball one hundred times in a row.
Instead, I consider the purchase of a stylish cane, one with an animal
head to hold in my aching hand. I've become cranky and rude. I eat
off paper plates, drink from plastic glasses. China and silver fade

under dust on the shelves. I want to be back where I was before.
I want to wrap my legs around another body. I want to earn hard
breathing. I want to build my own garden wall, bend to place
seeds in the black earth with my own hand. I want to wake

in the quiet morning glad for the day in front of me and the dreams
behind. I want to lie in the sun all long afternoon, hot and easy and
dazed by good fortune. I want to bicycle down the hill with Elizabeth.
How do others move through this with such grace and good manners?

My days are short as winter solstice, even in summer heat. I have no desire left, except for sleep, solitude, a feathered bed. No, sorry, I'm too tired, too many people at parties, too much noise in the streets. There is no prince. There is no heaven. There is no sleep.

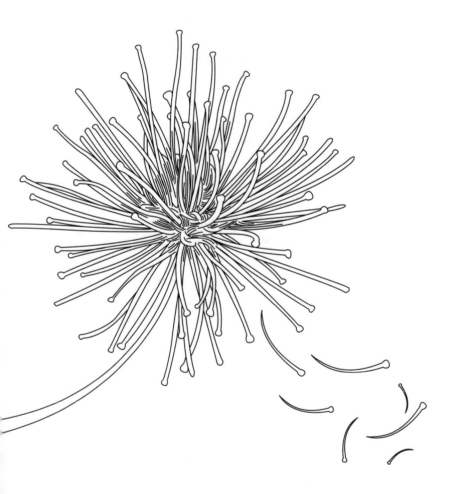

A Mary F Robinson
(1857-1944)

Neurasthenia

I watch the happier people of the house
    Come in and out, and talk, and go their ways;
I sit and gaze at them; I cannot rouse
    My heavy mind to share their busy days.

I watch them glide, like skaters on a stream,
    Across the brilliant surface of the world.
But I am underneath: they do not dream
    How deep below the eddying flood is whirl'd.

They cannot come to me, nor I to them;
    But, if a mightier arm could reach and save,
Should I forget the tide I had to stem?
    Should I, like these, ignore the abysmal wave?

Yes! in the radiant air how could I know
How black it is, how fast it is, below?

Jane Cave
(*c* 1754-1813)

from

The Head-Ache,
or An Ode to Health

Ah! why from me art thou for ever flown?
Why deaf to every agonising groan?
Not one short month for ten revolving years,
But pain within my frame its sceptre rears!
In each successive month full twelve long days
And tedious nights my sun withdraws his rays!
Leaves me in silent anguish on my bed,
Afflicting all the members in the head;
Through every particle the torture flies,
But centres in the temples, brain, and eyes;
The efforts of the hands and feet are vain,
While bows the head with agonising pain;
While heaves the breast th' unutterable sigh,
And the big tear drops from the languid eye.
For ah! my children want a mother's care,
A husband too should due assistance share;
Myself, for action formed, would fain through life
Be found th' assiduous, valuable wife;
But now, behold, I live unfit for aught;
Inactive half my days except in thought,
And this so vague while torture clogs my hours,
I sigh, 'Oh, twill derange my mental powers,
Or by its dire excess dissolve my sight,
And thus entomb me in perpetual night!'

Carole Satyamurti
(*b* 1939)

from

Changing the Subject

Diagnosis

He was good at telling,
gentle, but direct;
he stayed with me
while I recovered breath,
started to collect
stumbling questions. He said
cancer with a small c
– the raw stuff of routine –
yet his manner showed
he knew it couldn't be ordinary for me.
Walking down the road
I shivered like a gong
that's just been struck
– mutilation … what have I done …
my child … how long …
– and noticed how
the vast possible array
of individual speech
is whittled by bad news
to what all frightened people say.
That night, the freak storm.
I listened to trees fall,
stout fences crack,
felt the house shudder as the wind
howled the truest cliché of them all.

Pauline

Six years ago, refused surgery
– liked her breasts,
wasn't going to be cut up.

Three years ago,
her liver affected,
the doctor talked of a few months,

but she wasn't going to die
with her son away in Africa
– not for two years at least.

She swam a lot, played bridge,
visited the sick,
went to car-maintenance classes.

Last month, a funny turn
– it's reached her brain.
She'd worried she was going mad!

So here she is, in the bed opposite,
going for radiotherapy,
losing her hair.

She sits upright,
excited, laughing,
choosing a wig from a big box.

Multitudes of flowers, cards,
friends of different ages, sexes,
colours, crowd around.

Her husband, who always hopes
to have her to himself,
sulks behind The Times,

but she knows best.
Friends are security forces,
and she is in command.

How Are You?

When he asked me that
what if I'd said,
rather than 'very well',
'dreadful – full of dread'?

Since I have known this
language has cracked,
meanings have re-arranged;
dream, risk and fact

changed places. Tenses tip,
word-roots are suddenly
important, some grip
on the slippery.

We're on thin linguistic ice
lifelong, but I see through;
I read the sentence
we all are subject to

in the stopped mouths of those
who once were 'I',
full-fleshed, confident
using the verb 'to die'

of plants and pets and parents
until the immense
contingency of things
deleted sense.

They are his future
as well as mine,
but I won't make him look.
I say, 'I'm fine.'

Jan Williams
(*b* 1953)

Loss

I have left you and gone to another place
And you are angry with me.
I have let you down, I have deceived you.
I am not the vibrant woman you once loved.
I am sick and I inhabit the land of the sick.
I've lived here now for five long years.
The terrain is harsh and punishing,
Yet it has its own savage beauty
And I've learned the language and I know the people.
But I miss you.

Each morning I walk down to the border crossing
And look out for you.
And when I catch sight of you, I call your name
And reach out my hands.
You turn for a moment and look at me.
But your world is calling more loudly, more insistently.
You turn away again and I die a little more.
I have left you and gone to the land of the sick
And you cannot forgive me.
And I cannot forgive myself.

Emily Dickinson
(1830-86)

There is a pain – so utter

There is a pain – so utter –
It swallows substance up –
Then covers the Abyss with Trance –
So Memory can step
Around – across – upon it –
As one within a Swoon –
Goes safely – where an open eye –
Would drop Him – Bone by Bone.

Elizabeth Jennings
(1926-2001)

Pain

At my wits' end
And all resources gone, I lie here,
All of my body tense to the touch of fear,
And all my mind,

Muffled now as if the nerves
Refused any longer to let thoughts form,
Is no longer a safe retreat, a tidy home,
No longer serves

My body's demands or shields
With fine words, as it once would daily,
My storehouse of dread. Now, slowly,
My heart, hand, whole body yield

To fear. Bed, ward, window begin
To lose their solidity. Faces no longer
Look kind or needed; yet I still fight the stronger
Terror – oblivion – the needle thrusts in.

W E Henley
(1849-1903)

Vigil

Lived on one's back
In the long hours of repose,
Life is a practical nightmare –
Hideous asleep or awake.

Shoulders and loins
Ache — !
Ache, and the mattress,
Run into boulders and hummocks,
Glows like a kiln, while the bedclothes –
Tumbling, importunate, daft –
Ramble and roll, and the gas,   *[lighting*
Screwed to its lowermost,
An inevitable atom of light,
Haunts, and a stertorous sleeper
Snores me to hate and despair.

All the old time
Surges malignant before me;
Old voices, old kisses, old songs
Blossom derisive about me;
While the new days
Pass me in endless procession:
A pageant of shadows

Silently, leeringly wending
On . . . and still on . . . still on!

Far in the stillness a cat
Languishes loudly. A cinder
Falls, and the shadows
Lurch to the leap of the flame. The next man to me
Turns with a moan; and the snorer,
The drug like a rope at his throat,
Gasps, gurgles, snorts himself free, as the night-nurse,
Noiseless and strange,
Her bull's eye half-lanterned in apron,   [*lamp*
(Whispering me, 'Are ye no' sleepin' yet?'),
Passes, list-slippered and peering,   [*soft-soled*
Round . . . and is gone.

Sleep comes at last –
Sleep full of dreams and misgivings –
Broken with brutal and sordid
Voices and sounds that impose on me,
Ere I can wake to it,
The unnatural, intolerable day.

Emily Dickinson
(1830-86)

I felt a cleavage in my mind

I felt a cleavage in my mind
      As if my brain had split;
I tried to match it, seam by seam,
      But could not make them fit.

The thought behind I strove to join
      Unto the thought before,
But sequence ravelled out of reach
      Like balls upon a floor.

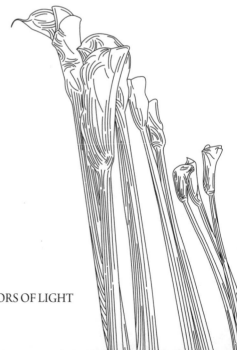

John Clare
(1793-1864)

I Am

I am; yet what I am none cares or knows,
My friends forsake me like a memory lost;
I am the self-consumer of my woes,
They rise and vanish in oblivious host,
Like shades in love and death's oblivion lost;
And yet I am, and live with shadows tost

Into the nothingness of scorn and noise,
Into the living sea of waking dreams,
Where there is neither sense of life nor joys,
But the vast shipwreck of my life's esteems;
And e'en the dearest – that I loved the best –
Are strange – nay, rather stranger than the rest.

I long for scenes where man has never trod,
A place where woman never smiled or wept;
There to abide with my Creator, God,
And sleep as I in childhood sweetly slept:
Untroubling and untroubled where I lie,
The grass below – above the vaulted sky.

Gerda Mayer
(*b* 1927)

The Man on the Desert Island

The man on the desert island
Has forgotten the ways of people,
His stories are all of himself.
Day in, day out of time
He communes with himself and sends
Messages in green bottles:
Help me *they say* I am
Cast up and far from home.
Each day he goes to watch
The horizon for ships.
Nothing reaches his shore
Except corked green bottles.

David Lees
(*b* 1954)

Written in Sickness

Each day's work is holding back despair
As precious years drift by and disappear;
How long will I find strength enough to bear?

Unaged but decaying, like a pear
Unripe and green when rot and mould appear;
Each day's work is holding back despair.

In limbo now, I make plans as I dare,
But sickness smothers each new-born idea;
How long will I find strength enough to bear?

Friends see no desperate man in my wheelchair –
I banter, quip and join with their pale cheer;
But each day's work is holding back despair.

Night voices in the dark, comfortless air
Whisper 'Surrender' in my sleepless ear;
How long will I find strength enough to bear?

Oh, to give way, subside and cry 'Unfair
That I should live in sickness and in fear';
But each day's work is holding back despair:
How long will I find strength enough to bear?

Chidiock Tichborne
(*c* 1558-86)

Elegy for Himself
**written in the Tower before his execution
1586**

My prime of youth is but a frost of cares,
  My feast of joy is but a dish of pain,
My crop of corn is but a field of tares, [*weeds*
  And all my good is but vain hope of gain;
The day is past, and yet I saw no sun,
And now I live, and now my life is done.

My tale was heard, and yet it was not told,
  My fruit is fallen, and yet my leaves are green,
My youth is spent, and yet I am not old,
  I saw the world, and yet I was not seen;
My thread is cut, and yet it is not spun,
And now I live, and now my life is done.

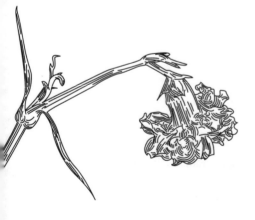

Ivor Gurney
(1890-1937)

To God

Why have you made life so intolerable
And set me between four walls, where I am able
Not to escape meals without prayer, for that is possible
Only by annoying an attendant. And tonight a sensual
Hell has been put on me, so that all has deserted me
And I am merely crying and trembling in heart
For Death, and cannot get it. And gone out is part
Of sanity. And there is dreadful Hell within me,
And nothing helps, forced meals there have been and electricity
And weakening of sanity by influence
That's dreadful to endure, and there is Orders
And I am praying for death, death, death
And dreadful is the indrawing or out-breathing of breath
Because of the intolerable insults put on my whole soul
Of the soul loathed, loathed, loathed of the soul.
Gone out every bright thing from my mind.
All lost that ever God himself designed.
Not half can be written of cruelty of man, on man,
Not often such evil guessed as between Man and Man.

Frances Cornford
(1886-1960)

The Watch

I wakened on my hot, hard bed,
Upon the pillow lay my head;
Beneath the pillow I could hear
My little watch was ticking clear.
I thought the throbbing of it went
Like my continual discontent;
I thought it said in every tick:
I am so sick, so sick, so sick;
O Death, come quick, come quick, come quick,
Come quick, come quick, come quick, come quick.

William Shakespeare
(1564-1616)

Oh that this too too solid Flesh would melt

HAMLET: Oh that this too too solid Flesh would melt,
Thaw, and resolve itself into a Dew!
Or that the Everlasting had not fix'd
His Canon 'gainst Selfe-slaughter! O God, O God!
How weary, stale, flat, and unprofitable
Seem to me all the uses of this world!
Fie on't! O fie, fie! 'tis an unweeded Garden
That growes to Seed: things rank and grosse in Nature
Possesse it meerely. That it should come to this!

Mary McCarthy

Lupus

Sickness is a place more instructive
than a long trip to Europe.
Flannery O'Connor

*The wolf rampages through my place;
his rage staggers on and on
untamed by any St Francis.*

*'A predisposition,' the doctor says;
medicine and disease struggle,
it is hard to tell them apart.*

*I journey alone with my inheritance,
learning to be at home
with who I am.*

Gwyneth Lewis
(*b* 1959)

Angel of Depression

Why would an angel choose to come here
if it weren't important? Into stuffy rooms
smelling of cabbage? Into the tedium of time,
which weighs like gravity on any messenger
used to more freedom and who has to wear
a dingy costume, so as not to scare
the humans. Wouldn't even an angel despair?

Don't say it's an honour to have fought
with depression's angel. It always wears
the face of my loved ones as it tears
the breath from my solar plexus, grinds
my face in the ever-resilient dirt.
Oh yes, I'm broken but my limp
is the best part of me. And the way I hurt.

Po Chu-ï
(772-846)
tr. Arthur Waley

Winter Night

My house is poor; those that I love have left me.
My body is sick; I cannot join the feast.
There is not a living soul before my eyes
As I lie alone locked in my cottage room.
My broken lamp burns with a feeble flame;
My tattered curtains are crooked and do not meet.
'Tsek, tsek' on the door-step and window-sill
Again I hear the new snow fall.
As I grow older, gradually I sleep less;
I wake at midnight and sit up straight in bed.
If I had not learned the 'art of sitting and forgetting',[1]
How could I bear this utter loneliness?
Stiff and stark my body cleaves to the earth;
Unimpeded my soul yields to Change.[2]
So it has been for four tedious years,
Through one thousand and three hundred nights!

---

[1] Buddhist meditation.
[2] The principle of endless mutation, which governs the Universe.

Jane Kenyon
(1947-95)

Now Where?

It wakes when I wake, walks
when I walk, turns back when I
turn back, beating me to the door.

It spoils my food and steals
my sleep, and mocks me, saying,
'Where is your God now?'

And so, like a widow, I lie down
after supper. If I lie down
or sit up it's all the same:

the days and nights bear me along.
To strangers I must seem
alive. Spring comes, summer;

cool clear weather; heat, rain…

William Blake
(1757-1827)

The Divine Image

To Mercy, Pity, Peace, and Love
All pray in their distress;
And to these virtues of delight
Return their thankfulness.

For Mercy, Pity, Peace, and Love
Is God, our father dear,
And Mercy, Pity, Peace, and Love
Is Man, his child and care.

For Mercy has a human heart,
Pity a human face,
And Love, the human form divine,
And Peace, the human dress.

Then every man, of every clime,
That prays in his distress,
Prays to the human form divine,
Love, Mercy, Pity, Peace.

And all must love the human form,
In heathen, Turk, or Jew;
Where Mercy, Love, and Pity dwell,
There God is dwelling too.

William J O'Malley
(*b* 1928)

Lord, I am tangled in a net of confusion and doubts

(after Psalm 31)

Lord, I am tangled in a net of confusion and doubts,
about myself, my friends, today, tomorrow – you.
My eyes are weary of weeping; my bones wither;
I am sick of feeling sorry for myself,
and those who know me are sickened by it, too.
I'm an unwelcome burden to them and to myself.
Heal me ! Heal me, even despite myself !
Make me remember that you have made me to live.
Help me to put myself aside
and see that what seems the wrath of God
is the love of God assessed by a fool.

William J O'Malley
(*b* 1928)

By the rivers of Babylon

(*after Psalm 137*)

By the rivers of Babylon we sat us down and wept,
surrendering our harps to the hands of weeping willows.
They plucked the strings and whispered,
'Sing! Sing of the yesteryears when you were young!'
How can I sing of the days when I was whole?
How can I sing in this unfocused wilderness?
How can I sing when the well of my heart is cracked
and barren of pity, even for myself?
Yahweh, I will take the harp of my soul into my hands.   [*Lord*
I will turn suffering to music, and I will sing!

John Fletcher
(1579-1625)

Weep no more

Weep no more, nor sigh, nor groan,
Sorrow calls no time that's gone: [brings back
Violets pluck'd, the sweetest rain
Makes not fresh nor grow again.
Trim thy locks, look cheerfully;
Fate's hid ends eyes cannot see.
Joys as wingèd dreams fly fast,
Why should sadness longer last?
Grief is but a wound to woe;
Gentlest fair, mourn, mourn no moe.   [more

PART II

IN A DARK TIME, THE EYE BEGINS TO SEE

John O'Donohue
(1956-2008)

For a Friend, on the Arrival of Illness

Now is the time of dark invitation
Beyond a frontier that you did not expect;
Abruptly, your old life seems distant.

You barely noticed how each day opened
A path through fields never questioned,
Yet expected, deep down, to hold treasure.
Now your time on earth becomes full of threat;
Before your eyes your future shrinks.

You lived absorbed in the day to day,
So continuous with everything around you,
That you could forget you were separate;

Now this dark companion has come between you,
Distances have opened in your eyes,
You feel that against your will
A stranger has married your heart.

Nothing before has made you
Feel so isolated and lost.

When the reverberations of shock subside in you,
May grace come to restore you to balance.
May it shape a new space in your heart
To embrace this illness as a teacher
Who has come to open your life to new worlds.

May you find in yourself
A courageous hospitality

Towards what is difficult,
Painful and unknown.

May you learn to use this illness
As a lantern to illuminate
The new qualities that will emerge in you.

May the fragile harvesting of this slow light
Help you to release whatever has become false in you.
May you trust this light to clear a path
Through all the fog of old unease and anxiety
Until you feel arising within you a tranquillity
Profound enough to call the storm to stillness.

May you find the wisdom to listen to your illness:
Ask it why it came? Why it chose your friendship?
Where it wants to take you? What it wants you to know?
What quality of space it wants to create in you?
What you need to learn to become more fully yourself
That your presence may shine in the world?

May you keep faith with your body,
Learning to see it as a holy sanctuary
Which can bring this night-wound gradually
Towards the healing and freedom of dawn.

May you be granted the courage and vision
To work through passivity and self-pity,
To see the beauty you can harvest
From the riches of this dark invitation.

May you learn to receive it graciously,
And promise to learn swiftly
That it may leave you newborn,
Willing to dedicate your time to birth.

Theodore Roethke
(1908-63)

In a Dark Time

In a dark time, the eye begins to see,
I meet my shadow in the deepening shade;
I hear my echo in the echoing wood –
A lord of nature weeping to a tree,
I live between the heron and the wren,
Beasts of the hill and serpents of the den.

What's madness but nobility of soul
At odds with circumstance? The day's on fire!
I know the purity of pure despair,
My shadow pinned against a sweating wall,
That place among the rocks – is it a cave,
Or winding path? The edge is what I have.

A steady storm of correspondences!
A night flowing with birds, a ragged moon,
And in broad day the midnight come again!
A man goes far to find out what he is –
Death of the self in a long, tearless night,
All natural shapes blazing unnatural light.

Dark, dark my light, and darker my desire.
My soul, like some heat-maddened summer fly,
Keeps buzzing at the sill. Which I is *I*?
A fallen man, I climb out of my fear.
The mind enters itself, and God the mind,
And one is One, free in the tearing wind.

Walt Whitman
(1819-92)

I think I could turn and live with animals

I think I could turn and live with animals, they are
*   so placid and self-contain'd,*
I stand and look at them long and long.

They do not sweat and whine about their condition,
They do not lie awake in the dark and weep for their sins,
They do not make me sick discussing their duty to God,
Not one is dissatisfied, not one is demented with
*   the mania of owning things,*
Not one kneels to another, nor to his kind that lived
*   thousands of years ago,*
Not one is respectable or unhappy over the whole earth.

Dannie Abse
(*b* 1923)

A Wall

in a field in the County of Glamorgan.
You won't find it named in any guidebook.
It lies, plonk, in the middle of rising ground,
forty-four paces long, high as your eyes,
it begins for no reason, ends no place.
No other walls are adjacent to it.
Seemingly unremarkable, it's just there,
stones of different sizes, different greys.

Don't say this wall is useless, that the grass
on the shadow side is much like the other.
It exists for golden lichens to settle,
for butterflies in their obstacle race
chasing each other to the winning post,
for huddling sheep in a slanting rainfall,
for you to say, 'This wall is beautiful.'

Tomas Tranströmer
(*b* 1931)
tr. Robin Fulton

Tracks

2 a.m.: moonlight. The train has stopped
out in the middle of the plain. Far away, points of light in a town,
flickering coldly at the horizon.

As when someone has gone into a dream so deep
he'll never remember having been there
when he comes back to his room.

As when someone has gone into an illness so deep
everything his days were becomes a few flickering points, a swarm,
cold and tiny at the horizon.

The train is standing quite still.
2 a.m.: bright moonlight, few stars.

Walt Whitman
(1819-92)

A noiseless patient spider

A noiseless patient spider,
I mark'd where on a little promontory it stood isolated,
Mark'd how to explore the vacant vast surrounding,
It launch'd forth filament, filament, filament, out of itself,
Ever unreeling them, ever tirelessly speeding them.

And you O my soul where you stand,
Surrounded, detached, in measureless oceans of space,
Ceaselessly musing, venturing, throwing, seeking the spheres
*   to connect them;*
Till the bridge you will need be form'd, till the ductile anchor hold,
Till the gossamer thread you fling catch somewhere, O my soul.

Mary Oliver
(*b* 1935)

Wild Geese

You do not have to be good.
You do not have to walk on your knees
for a hundred miles through the desert, repenting.
You only have to let the soft animal of your body
     love what it loves.
Tell me about despair, yours, and I will tell you mine.
Meanwhile the world goes on.
Meanwhile the sun and the clear pebbles of the rain
are moving across the landscapes,
over the prairies and the deep trees,
the mountains and the rivers.
Meanwhile the wild geese, high in the clean blue air,
are heading home again.
Whoever you are, no matter how lonely,
the world offers itself to your imagination,
calls to you like the wild geese, harsh and exciting –
over and over announcing your place
in the family of things.

Rainer Maria Rilke
(1875-1926)
tr. Robert Bly

Sunset

Slowly the west reaches for clothes of new colours
which it passes to a row of ancient trees.
You look, and soon these two worlds both leave you,
one part climbs toward heaven, one sinks to earth,

leaving you, not really belonging to either,
not so helplessly dark as that house that is silent,
not so unswervingly given to the eternal as that thing
that turns to a star each night and climbs –

leaving you (it is impossible to untangle the threads)
your own life, timid and standing high and growing,
so that, sometimes blocked in, sometimes reaching out,
one moment your life is a stone in you, and the next, a star.

William Blake
(1757-1827)

Man was made for Joy & Woe

Man was made for Joy & Woe,
And when this we rightly know
Thro' the World we safely go.
Joy & Woe are woven fine,
A Clothing for the Soul divine:
Under every grief & pine
Runs a joy with silken twine.

Ella Wheeler Wilcox
(1850-1919)

from

Solitude

Laugh, and the world laughs with you;
 Weep, and you weep alone;
For the sad old earth must borrow its mirth,
 But has trouble enough of its own.
Sing, and the hills will answer;
 Sigh, it is lost on the air;
The echoes bound to a joyful sound,
 But shrink from voicing care.

Rejoice, and men will seek you;
 Grieve, and they turn and go;
They want full measure of all your pleasure,
 But they do not need your woe.
Be glad, and your friends are many;
 Be sad, and you lose them all. –
There are none to decline your nectared wine,
 But alone you must drink life's gall.

St Paul
(*c* 5-*c* 57)

(adapted from his First Letter to the Corinthians)

Love is …

Love is patient, and love is kind;
love is not jealous or boastful;
it is not arrogant or selfish or rude,
nor does it insist on its own way;
it does not take offence nor bear a grudge;
it does not condone wrongdoing,
but rejoices in the truth.

Love never gives up; it is always ready
to make allowances, to trust, to hope,
and to endure whatever comes.

Three things will last forever: faith, hope and love,
and the greatest of these is love.

Robert Frost
(1874-1963)

Stopping by Woods on a Snowy Evening

Whose woods these are I think I know.
His house is in the village though;
He will not see me stopping here
To watch his woods fill up with snow.

My little horse must think it queer
To stop without a farmhouse near
Between the woods and frozen lake
The darkest evening of the year.

He gives his harness bells a shake
To ask if there is some mistake.
The only other sound's the sweep
Of easy wind and downy flake.

The woods are lovely, dark and deep,
But I have promises to keep,
And miles to go before I sleep,
And miles to go before I sleep.

PART III

CURE ME WITH QUIETNESS

Ruth Pitter
(1897-1992)

Cure me with quietness

Cure me with quietness,
Bless me with peace;
Comfort my heaviness,
Stay me with ease.
Stillness in solitude
Send down like dew;
Mine armour of fortitude
Piece and make new:
That when I rise again
I may shine bright
As the sky after rain,
Day after night.

W B Yeats
(1865-1939)

The Lake Isle of Innisfree

I will arise and go now, and go to Innisfree,
And a small cabin build there, of clay and wattles made;
Nine bean-rows will I have there, a hive for the honey bee,
And live alone in the bee-loud glade.

And I shall have some peace there, for peace comes dropping slow,
Dropping from the veils of the morning to where the cricket sings;
There midnight's all a-glimmer, and noon a purple glow,
And evening full of the linnet's wings.

I will arise and go now, for always night and day
I hear lake water lapping with low sounds by the shore;
While I stand on the roadway, or on the pavements gray,
I hear it in the deep heart's core.

The island of Innisfree ('Heather Island') lies in Lough Gill in the north-west of Ireland.
The purple glow is the reflection of heather blossom on the water.

Wendell Berry
(b 1934)

The Peace of Wild Things

When despair for the world grows in me
and I wake in the night at the least sound
in fear of what my life and my children's lives may be,
I go and lie down where the wood drake
rests in his beauty on the water, and the great heron feeds.
I come into the peace of wild things
who do not tax their lives with forethought
of grief. I come into the presence of still water.
And I feel above me the day-blind stars
waiting with their light. For a time
I rest in the grace of the world, and am free.

Coventry Patmore
(1823-96)

Magna Est Veritas[1]

Here, in this little Bay,
Full of tumultuous life and great repose,
Where, twice a day,
The purposeless, glad ocean comes and goes,
Under high cliffs, and far from the huge town,
I sit me down.
For want of me the world's course will not fail:
When all its work is done, the lie shall rot;
The truth is great, and shall prevail,
When none cares whether it prevail or not.

---

[1] *Magna est veritas et praevalet* ('Great is truth and it prevails') – 1 Esdras 4:41 (Vulgate Bible).

William Soutar
(1898-1943)

The Room

Into the quiet of this room
Words from the clamorous world come:
The shadows of the gesturing year
Quicken upon the stillness here.

The wandering waters do not mock
The pool within its wall of rock
But turn their healing tides and come
Even as the day into this room.

Molly Holden
(1927-81)

Proverb

I am determined not to miss
one nuance of the light
on spire and tree
this bright September evening.
So I sit and stare,
the washing-up undone, the cat
unfed, watching the sunset penetrate
pinnacle and bell-tower louvre
of the church, fine-fingered leaves
and conker cases of the golden tree.

The oak's oil-brown, the ash
still green. The grass I cannot see
must strike up damp but rosy-crowned
with the last sunlight
slanting down the hill. I cannot
go out into that evening but my spies,
memory and imagination,
report back faithfully. I recall
the Chinese proverb about selling
half of one's last loaf to buy
flowers for the soul but I wonder,
if I had the choice now, whether
I'd have longer years of ordinary life
or this half-life and the tingle
of senses extra-sharp to beauty
as now sit contemplating dusk.

Elizabeth Bishop
(1911-79)

I am in need of music

I am in need of music that would flow
Over my fretful, feeling finger-tips,
Over my bitter-tainted, trembling lips,
With melody, deep, clear, and liquid-slow.
Oh, for the healing swaying, old and low,
Of some song sung to rest the tired dead,
A song to fall like water on my head,
And over quivering limbs, dream flushed to glow!

There is a magic made by melody:
A spell of rest, and quiet breath, and cool
Heart, that sinks through fading colors deep
To the subaqueous stillness of the sea,
And floats forever in a moon-green pool,
Held in the arms of rhythm and of sleep.

Alfred Tennyson
(1809-92)

from

The Lotos-Eaters

There is sweet music here that softer falls
Than petals from blown roses on the grass,
Or night-dews on still waters between walls
Of shadowy granite, in a gleaming pass;
Music that gentlier on the spirit lies,
Than tir'd eyelids upon tir'd eyes;
Music that brings sweet sleep down from the blissful skies.
Here are cool mosses deep,
And through the moss the ivies creep,
And in the stream the long-leaved flowers weep,
And from the craggy ledge the poppy hangs in sleep.

John Fletcher
(1579-1625)

Care-charming Sleep

Care-charming Sleep, thou easer of all woes,
Brother to Death, sweetly thyself dispose
On this afflicted prince; fall like a cloud
In gentle showers; give nothing that is loud
Or painful to his slumbers; easy, sweet,
And as a purling stream, thou son of Night,
Pass by his troubled senses; sing his pain,
Like hollow murmuring wind, or silver rain;
Into this prince gently, oh gently slide,
And kiss him into slumbers like a bride.

Siegfried Sassoon
(1886-1967)

Falling Asleep

Voices moving about in the quiet house:
Thud of feet and a muffled shutting of doors:
Everyone yawning. Only the clocks are alert.

Out in the night there's autumn-smelling gloom
Crowded with whispering trees; across the park
A hollow cry of hounds like lonely bells:
And I know that the clouds are moving across the moon;
The low, red, rising moon. Now herons call
And wrangle by their pool; and hooting owls
Sail from the wood above pale stooks of oats.

Waiting for sleep, I drift from thoughts like these;
And where to-day was dream-like, build my dreams.
Music ... there was a bright white room below,
And someone singing a song about a soldier,
One hour, two hours ago: and soon the song
Will be 'last night': but now the beauty swings
Across my brain, ghost of remembered chords
Which still can make such radiance in my dream
That I can watch the marching of my soldiers,
And count their faces; faces, sunlit faces.

Falling asleep ... the herons, and the hounds ... .
September in the darkness; and the world
I've known; all fading past me into peace.

Po Chu-ï
(772-846)
tr. Arthur Waley

Being Visited by a Friend during Illness

I have been ill so long that I do not count the days;
At the southern window, evening – and again evening.
Sadly chirping in the grasses under my eaves
The winter sparrows morning and evening sing.
By an effort I rise and lean heavily on my bed;
Tottering I step towards the door of the courtyard.
By chance I meet a friend who is coming to see me;
Just as if I had gone specially to meet him.
They took my couch and placed it in the setting sun;
They spread my rug and I leaned on the balcony-pillar.
Tranquil talk was better than any medicine;
Gradually the feelings came back to my numbed heart.

Dinah Maria Craik
(1826-87)

Friendship

Oh, the comfort –
the inexpressible comfort of feeling *safe* with a person –
having neither to weigh thoughts nor measure words,
but pouring them all right out,
just as they are,
chaff and grain together;
certain that a faithful hand will take and sift them,
keep what is worth keeping,
and then with the breath of kindness blow the rest away.

Sasha Moorsom
(1931-93)

Jewels in My Hand

I hold dead friends like jewels in my hand
Watching their brilliance gleam against my palm
Turquoise and emerald, jade, a golden band.

All ravages of time they can withstand
Like talismans their grace keeps me from harm
I hold dead friends like jewels in my hand.

I see them standing in some borderland
Their hands half-turned, waiting to take my arm
Turquoise and emerald, jade, a golden band.

I'm not afraid they will misunderstand
My turning to them like a magic charm
I hold dead friends like jewels in my hand
Turquoise and emerald, jade, a golden band.

William Shakespeare
(1564-1616)

Sonnet 30

When to the sessions of sweet silent thought
I summon up remembrance of things past,
I sigh the lack of many a thing I sought,
And with old woes new wail my dear time's waste:
Then can I drown an eye, unus'd to flow,
For precious friends hid in death's dateless night,
And weep afresh love's long-since cancell'd woe,
And moan the expense of many a vanish'd sight:
Then can I grieve at grievances foregone,
And heavily from woe to woe tell o'er
The sad account of fore-bemoaned moan,
Which I new pay as if not paid before.
    But if the while I think on thee, dear friend,
    All losses are restor'd, and sorrows end.

Oscar Hammerstein
(1895-1960)

You'll Never Walk Alone

When you walk through a storm,
Hold your head up high
And don't be afraid of the dark;

At the end of the storm
Is a golden sky
And the sweet silver song of a lark.

Walk on through the wind,
Walk on through the rain,
Though your dreams be tossed and blown;

Walk on, walk on with hope in your heart
And you'll never walk alone,
You'll never walk alone;

Walk on, walk on with hope in your heart,
And you'll never walk alone,
You'll never walk alone.

Thomas Hood
(1799-1845)

I Remember, I Remember

I remember, I remember,
The house where I was born,
The little window where the sun
Came peeping in at morn;
He never came a wink too soon
Nor brought too long a day;
But now, I often wish the night
Had borne my breath away.

I remember, I remember
The roses red and white,
The violets, and the lily cups,
Those flowers made of light!
The lilacs where the robin built,
And where my brother set
The laburnum on his birth-day, –
The tree is living yet!

I remember, I remember
Where I was used to swing,
And thought the air must rush as fresh
To swallows on the wing;

My spirit flew in feathers then
That is so heavy now,
And summer pools could hardly cool
The fever on my brow!

I remember, I remember
The fir-trees dark and high;
I used to think their slender tops
Were close against the sky:
It was a childish ignorance,
But now 'tis little joy
To know I'm farther off from heav'n
Than when I was a boy.

Dylan Thomas
(1914-53)

Fern Hill

Now as I was young and easy under the apple boughs
About the lilting house and happy as the grass was green,
    The night above the dingle starry,
       Time let me hail and climb
     Golden in the heydays of his eyes,
And honoured among wagons I was prince of the apple towns
And once below a time I lordly had the trees and leaves
       Trail with daisies and barley
    Down the rivers of the windfall light.

And as I was green and carefree, famous among the barns
About the happy yard and singing as the farm was home,
    In the sun that is young once only,
       Time let me play and be
     Golden in the mercy of his means,
And green and golden I was huntsman and herdsman, the calves
Sang to my horn, the foxes on the hills barked clear and cold,
       And the sabbath rang slowly
    In the pebbles of the holy streams.

All the sun long it was running, it was lovely, the hay
Fields high as the house, the tunes from the chimneys, it was air
    And playing, lovely and watery
       And fire green as grass.

And nightly under the simple stars
As I rode to sleep the owls were bearing the farm away,
All the moon long I heard, blessed among stables, the nightjars
        Flying with the ricks, and the horses
            Flashing into the dark.

And then to awake, and the farm, like a wanderer white
With the dew, come back, the cock on his shoulder: it was all
        Shining, it was Adam and maiden,
            The sky gathered again
        And the sun grew round that very day.
So it must have been after the birth of the simple light
In the first, spinning place, the spellbound horses walking warm
        Out of the whinnying green stable
            On to the fields of praise.

And honoured among foxes and pheasants by the gay house
Under the new made clouds and happy as the heart was long,
        In the sun born over and over,
            I ran my heedless ways,
        My wishes raced through the house high hay
And nothing I cared, at my sky blue trades, that time allows
In all his tuneful turning so few and such morning songs
        Before the children green and golden
            Follow him out of grace,

Nothing I cared, in the lamb white days, that time would take me
Up to the swallow thronged loft by the shadow of my hand,
   In the moon that is always rising,
         Nor that riding to sleep
      I should hear him fly with the high fields
And wake to the farm forever fled from the childless land.
Oh as I was young and easy in the mercy of his means,
         Time held me green and dying
      Though I sang in my chains like the sea.

PART IV

LOOK TO THIS DAY

Anonymous

Look to this day

Look to this day,
For it is life, the very life of life.
In its brief course
Lie all the verities and realities of your existence –
The bliss of growth,
The glory of action,
The splendour of achievement,
Are but experiences of time.
For yesterday is but a dream
And tomorrow is only a vision;
And today well-lived makes
Yesterday a dream of happiness
And every tomorrow a vision of hope.
Look well therefore to this day:
Such is the salutation to the ever-new dawn !

E E Cummings
(1894-1962)

i thank You God

i thank You God for most this amazing
day: for the leaping greenly spirits of trees
and a blue true dream of sky;and for everything
which is natural which is infinite which is yes

(i who have died am alive again today,
and this is the sun's birthday;this is the birth
day of life and of love and wings:and of the gay
great happening illimitably earth)

how should tasting touching hearing seeing
breathing any—lifted from the no
of all nothing—human merely being
doubt unimaginable You?

(now the ears of my ears awake and
now the eyes of my eyes are opened)

W E Henley

(1849-1903)

Invictus

Out of the night that covers me,
    Black as the Pit from pole to pole,
I thank whatever gods may be
    For my unconquerable soul.

In the fell clutch of circumstance
    I have not winced nor cried aloud.
Under the bludgeonings of chance
    My head is bloody, but unbowed.

Beyond this place of wrath and tears
    Looms but the Horror of the shade,
And yet the menace of the years
    Finds and shall find me unafraid.

It matters not how strait the gate,
    How charged with punishments the scroll,
I am the master of my fate:
    I am the captain of my soul.

John Bunyan
(1628-88)

Who would true Valour see

Who would true Valour see
Let him come hither;
One here will Constant be,
Come Wind, come Weather.
There's no Discouragement
Shall make him once Relent
His first avow'd Intent
To be a Pilgrim.

Who so beset him round,
With dismal Stories,
Do but themselves Confound;
His Strength the more is.
No Lyon can him fright,
He'll with a Giant Fight,
But he will have a right
To be a Pilgrim.

Hobgoblin, nor foul Fiend,
Can daunt his Spirit:
He knows, he at the end,
Shall Life Inherit.
Then Fancies fly away,
He'll fear not what men say,
He'll labour Night and Day
To be a Pilgrim.

Anonymous

Sometimes

Sometimes things don't go, after all,
from bad to worse. Some years, muscadel
faces down frost; green thrives; the crops don't fail.
Sometimes a man aims high, and all goes well.

A people sometimes will step back from war;
elect an honest man; decide they care
enough, that they can't leave some stranger poor.
Some men become what they were born for.

Sometimes our best efforts do not go
amiss; sometimes we do as we meant to.
The sun will sometimes melt a field of sorrow
that seemed hard frozen; may it happen for you.

Victoria Flute
(*b* 1978)

On Hold

The cure you would like to have
is currently unavailable.
Please try again later.

The life you are trying to reach
knows you are waiting.
Please hold.

Your hopes are important to us –
we will be with you shortly.
Please hang on.

Sheila Gay

The sun is there

The sun is there –
the sun **is** there,
but clouds are in the way –

clouds that sadness makes
out of fragments of your broken life,
the turning off of joy,
the shattered memory of better days
when pain and suffering were strangers to you
and tears were simply rainy weather –

but still the sun is there,
its warmth still glowing in your family's love,
the constancy of friends,
the unexpected kindnesses,
in good times and in bad –

the sun **is** there !

Derek Walcott
(*b* 1930)

Love after Love

The time will come
when, with elation,
you will greet yourself arriving
at your own door, in your own mirror,
and each will smile at the other's welcome,

and say, sit here. Eat.
You will love again the stranger who was your self.
Give wine. Give bread. Give back your heart
to itself, to the stranger who has loved you

all your life, whom you ignored
for another, who knows you by heart.
Take down the love letters from the bookshelf,

the photographs, the desperate notes,
peel your own image from the mirror.
Sit. Feast on your life.

James Kirkup
(1918-2009)

There is a new morning

There is a new morning, and a new way,
When the heart wakes in the green
Meadow of its choice, and the feet stray
Securely on their new-found paths, unseen,
Unhindered in the certain light of day.

There is a new time, and a new word
That is the timeless dream of uncreated speech.
When the heart beats for the first time, like a bird
Battering the bright boughs of its tree; when each
To the other turns, all prayers are heard.

There is a new world, and a new man
Who walks amazed that he so long
Was blind, and dumb; he who now towards the sun
Lifts up a trustful face in skilful song,
And fears no more the darkness where his day began.

Philip Larkin
(1922-85)

The Trees

The trees are coming into leaf
Like something almost being said;
The recent buds relax and spread,
Their greenness is a kind of grief.

Is it that they are born again
And we grow old? No, they die too.
Their yearly trick of looking new
Is written down in rings of grain.

Yet still the unresting castles thresh
In fullgrown thickness every May.
Last year is dead, they seem to say,
Begin afresh, afresh, afresh.

W B Yeats
(1865-1939)

The Song of Wandering Aengus

I went out to the hazel wood,
Because a fire was in my head,
And cut and peeled a hazel wand,
And hooked a berry to a thread;
And when white moths were on the wing,
And moth-like stars were flickering out,
I dropped the berry in a stream
And caught a little silver trout.

When I had laid it on the floor
I went to blow the fire a-flame,
But something rustled on the floor,
And someone called me by my name:
It had become a glimmering girl
With apple blossom in her hair
Who called me by my name and ran
And faded through the brightening air.

Though I am old with wandering
Through hollow lands and hilly lands,
I will find out where she has gone,
And kiss her lips and take her hands;
And walk among long dappled grass,
And pluck till time and times are done,
The silver apples of the moon,
The golden apples of the sun.

Aengus was the Irish god of love, youth, and poetic inspiration.
In Celtic mythology the hazel represents creative wisdom.

Rabindranath Tagore
(1861-1941)

I thought that my voyage had come to its end

*I thought that my voyage had come to its end
at the last limit of my power, – that the path
before me was closed, that provisions
were exhausted and the time come
to take shelter in a silent obscurity.*

*But I find that Thy will knows no end in me.
And when old words die out on the tongue,
new melodies break forth from the heart;
and where the old tracks are lost,
new country is revealed with its wonders.*

D H Lawrence
(1885-1930)

Song of a Man who has Come Through

Not I, not I, but the wind that blows through me!
A fine wind is blowing the new direction of Time.
If only I let it bear me, carry me, if only it carry me!
If only I am sensitive, subtle, oh, delicate, a winged gift!
If only, most lovely of all, I yield myself and am borrowed
By the fine, fine wind that takes its course through the chaos
    of the world
Like a fine, an exquisite chisel, a wedge-blade inserted;
If only I am keen and hard like the sheer tip of a wedge
Driven by invisible blows,
The rock will split, we shall come at the wonder, we shall find
    the Hesperides.[1]

Oh, for the wonder that bubbles into my soul,
I would be a good fountain, a good well-head,
Would blur no whisper, spoil no expression.

What is the knocking?
What is the knocking at the door in the night?
It is somebody wants to do us harm.

No, no, it is the three strange angels.
Admit them, admit them.

---

[1] In Greek mythology, the three nymphs who tend a blissful, enchanted garden in the west
where golden apples grow, the source of the evening light of sunset.

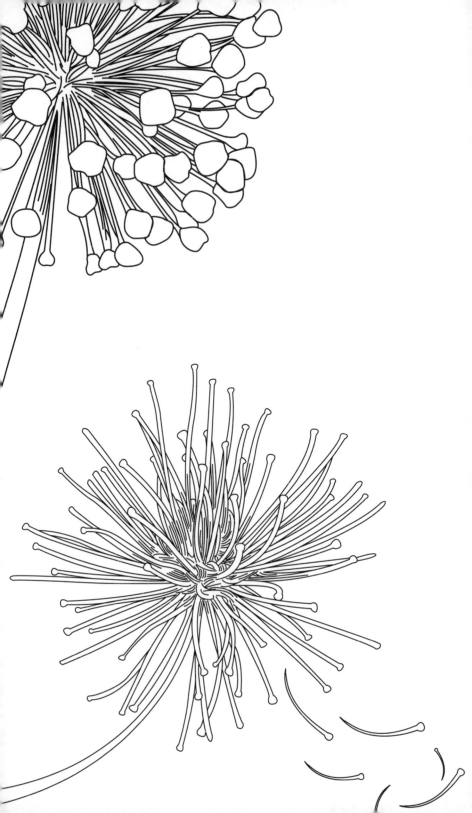

PART V

SEASONS OF BEAUTY AND HOPE

Mary Mestecky
(*b* 1938)

Dreamcoat

See! There! In the middle of the row!
That's my coat glowing among drab winter garments –
My magic coat holding summer in its paisleyed pathways
To the rose gardens of Shalimar,
Where the spice winds blow.

I wear it for Omnipotence, my coat of dreams;
Languid on velvet cushions I raise my flowered arm
In benediction – and my people smile:
I am Woman and Mystery.
Men from ivory towers prostrate themselves before me
But I step splendid over them along sea-paths
Where ships flash silver oars, or purple sails
Swell in the silken winds.

I tell the tales caught in the threads
Of its shimmering fabric:
I summon ogres and heroes to the clash of battle
And stars to dance for me in night-perfumed gardens;
How damsels snare knights with golden nets of hair –
Ride with them bareback through enchanted forests
To castles drifting through high clouds.

Look! There on the peg my coat can work its magic
Drawing the inner eye away from winter
To summer, bright with imagination.

Anonymous
(14th Century, modernised)

Spring

Spring is come with love to town
With blossom and with birdsong
    Which this blissful season brings;
Daisies in the dales,
The sweet notes of nightingales –
    Each bird differently sings;
The throstelcock[1] chides endlessly;
Gone is winter's woe
    When up the woodruff springs;
The birds sing prodigiously
And carol of their wealth of joy
    So that all the woodland rings.

The rose puts on her blush;
The leaves on the bright branch
    Burgeon with a will;
The moon sends forth her silver light;
The lily is lovely to see,
    As are the fennel and the chervil;
The wild drakes begin to woo;
All creatures rejoice in their mates,
    As a stream that gently flows;

---

[1] The song thrush.

An ardent man sighs, as do many others,
For love that goes awry –
    I know, I'm one of those.

The moon radiates her lustre,
As does the lovely bright sun
    When the birds sing so gloriously;
Dews drench the downs,
Creatures make their choices
    With sounds murmured secretly;
Worms mate underground,
Women grow wonderfully proud –
    Spring suits them perfectly;
If I should fail to gain the love of one
I'll forgo all this wealth of joy
    And into the forest I'll flee.

Kathleen Raine
(1908-2003)

April's new apple buds

April's new apple buds on an old lichened tree;
Slender shadows quiver, celandines burn in the orchard grass –
This moment's image: how long does a moment stay?
I look, and look away, and look again, and see
The morning light has changed a little,
        the linnet flown; but who can say
When one moment's present became the next moment's past
To which this now was still the yet-to-be?
It seems, in this old walled garden, time does not pass,
Only mind wanders and returns; I watch attentively
And see not one green blade move out of its place.
The Easter daffodils, the shadows and the apple-trees
Phrases in music continuous from first to last.
To be is to be always here and now.
The green linnet flits from bough to bough.

Robert Browning
(1812-89)

Home Thoughts, from Abroad

Oh, to be in England
Now that April's there,
And whoever wakes in England
Sees, some morning, unaware,
That the lowest boughs and the brushwood sheaf
Round the elm-tree bole are in tiny leaf,
While the chaffinch sings on the orchard bough
In England – now!

And after April, when May follows,
And the whitethroat builds, and all the swallows!
Hark, where my blossom'd pear-tree in the hedge
Leans to the field and scatters on the clover
Blossoms and dewdrops – at the bent spray's edge –
That's the wise thrush; he sings each song twice over,
Lest you should think he never could recapture
The first fine careless rapture!
And though the fields look rough with hoary dew,
All will be gay when noontide wakes anew
The buttercups, the little children's dower
– Far brighter than this gaudy melon-flower!

Matthew Arnold
(1822-88)

Soon will the high Midsummer pomps come on

Soon will the high Midsummer pomps come on,
    Soon will the musk carnations break and swell,
Soon shall we have gold-dusted snapdragon,
    Sweet-William with his homely cottage-smell,
        And stocks in fragrant blow;
Roses that down the alleys shine afar,
    And open, jasmine-muffled lattices,
    And groups under the dreaming garden-trees,
And the full moon, and the white evening-star.

Edith Nesbit
(1858-1924)

Summer Song

There are white moon daisies in the mist of the meadow
Where the flowered grass scatters its seeds like spray,
There are purple orchis by the wood-ways' shadow,
There are pale dog-roses by the white highway;
And the grass, the grass is tall, the grass is up for hay,
With daisies white like silver and buttercups like gold,
And it's oh! for once to play thro' the long, the lovely day,
To laugh before the year grows old!

There is silver moonlight on the breast of the river
Where the willows tremble to the kiss of night,
Where the nine tall aspens in the meadow shiver,
Shiver in the night wind that turns them white.
And the lamps, the lamps are lit, the lamps are glow-worms' light,
Between the silver aspens and the west's last gold.
And it's oh! to drink delight in the lovely lonely night,
To be young before the heart grows old!

Vernon Scannell
(1922-2007)

from

The Long and Lovely Summers

How long and lovely were the summers then,
Each misted morning verdant milk, until
The sun blurred through, at first a pallid wen
Beneath the sky's bland skin and then, still pale,
A swollen, silvery dahlia-head, before
It burned to gold on laundered gentian blue.

At noon the picnic by the waterfall,
The bright behaviour of the butterflies
Interpreting the light; the plover's call
Above the rhyming flowers, the sun-baked pies
Of cow-pats, fossilized, antique; the cool
Shades of chestnuts, little pools of night.

Night: frosted mathematics of the stars;
Homages of fragrances; the moon,
Curved kukri-blade of ice; the green guitars
And soft soprano breeze conspired to croon
Late lullabies that soothed us into dream
And on to dawn which new delights would spice.

Henry Longfellow
(1807-82)

from

Rain in Summer

How beautiful is the rain!
After the dust and heat,
In the broad and fiery street,
In the narrow lane,
How beautiful is the rain!

How it clatters along the roofs,
Like the tramp of hoofs!
How it gushes and struggles out
From the throat of the overflowing spout!

Across the window-pane
It pours and pours;
And swift and wide,
With a muddy tide,
Like a river down the gutter roars
The rain, the welcome rain!

The sick man from his chamber looks
At the twisted brooks;
He can feel the cool
Breath of each little pool;
His fevered brain
Grows calm again,
And he breathes a blessing on the rain.

Gerard Manley Hopkins
(1844-89)

Hurrahing in Harvest

Summer ends now; now, barbarous in beauty, the stooks rise
    Around; up above, what wind-walks! what lovely behaviour
    Of silk-sack clouds! has wilder, wilful-wavier
Meal-drift moulded ever and melted across skies?

I walk, I lift up, I lift up heart, eyes,
    Down all that glory in the heavens to glean our Saviour;
    And eyes, heart, what looks, what lips yet give you a
Rapturous love's greeting of realer, of rounder replies?

And the azurous hung hills are his world-wielding shoulder
    Majestic – as a stallion stalwart, very-violet-sweet! –
These things, these things were here and but the beholder
    Wanting; which two when they once meet,
The heart rears wings bold and bolder
    And hurls for him, O half hurls earth for him off under his feet.

Emily Dickinson
(1830-86)

As imperceptibly as Grief

As imperceptibly as Grief
The Summer lapsed away –
Too imperceptible at last
To seem like Perfidy –
A Quietness distilled
As Twilight long begun,
Or Nature spending with herself
Sequestered Afternoon –
The Dusk drew earlier in –
The Morning foreign shone –
A courteous, yet harrowing Grace,
As Guest, that would be gone –
And thus, without a Wing,
Or service of a Keel
Our Summer made her light escape
Into the Beautiful.

Laurence Binyon
(1869-1943)

The Burning of the Leaves

Now is the time for the burning of the leaves.
They go to the fire; the nostrils prick with smoke
Wandering slowly into a weeping mist.
Brittle and blotched, ragged and rotten sheaves!
A flame seizes the smouldering ruin and bites
On stubborn stalks that crackle as they resist.

The last hollyhock's fallen tower is dust;
All the spices of June are a bitter reek,
All the extravagant riches spent and mean.
All burns! the reddest rose is a ghost;
Sparks whirl up, to expire in the mist: the wild
Fingers of fire are making corruption clean.

Now is the time for stripping the spirit bare,
Time for the burning of days ended and done,
Idle solace of things that have gone before:
Rootless hope and fruitless desire are there;
Let them go to the fire, with never a look behind.
That world that was ours is a world that is ours no more.

They will come again, the leaf and the flower, to arise
From squalor of rottenness into the old splendour,
And magical scents to a wondering memory bring;
The same glory, to shine upon different eyes.
Earth cares for her own ruins, naught for ours.
Nothing is certain, only the certain spring.

Robert Bridges
(1844-1930)

London Snow

When men were all asleep the snow came flying,
In large white flakes falling on the city brown,
Stealthily and perpetually settling and loosely lying,
    Hushing the latest traffic of the drowsy town;
Deadening, muffling, stifling its murmurs failing;
Lazily and incessantly floating down and down:
    Silently sifting and veiling road, roof and railing;
Hiding difference, making unevenness even,
Into angles and crevices softly drifting and sailing.
    All night it fell, and when full inches seven
It lay in the depth of its uncompacted lightness,
Its clouds blew off from a high and frosty heaven;
    And all woke earlier for the unaccustomed brightness
Of the winter dawning, the strange unheavenly glare:
The eye marvelled – marvelled at the dazzling whiteness;
    The ear hearkened to the stillness of the solemn air;
No sound of wheel rumbling nor of foot falling,
And the busy morning cries came thin and spare.
    Then boys I heard, as they went to school, calling,

They gathered up the crystal manna to freeze
Their tongues with tasting, their hands with snowballing;
    Or rioted in a drift, plunging up to the knees;
Or peering up from under the white-mossed wonder,
'O look at the trees!' they cried, 'O look at the trees!'

    With lessened load a few carts creak and blunder,
Following along the white deserted way,
A country company long dispersed asunder:
    When now already the sun, in pale display
Standing by Paul's high dome, spread forth below
His sparkling beams, and awoke the stir of the day.

    For now doors open, and war is waged with the snow;
And trains of sombre men, past tale of number,
Tread long brown paths, as toward their toil they go:
    But even for them awhile no cares encumber
Their minds diverted; the daily word is unspoken,
Their daily thoughts of labour and sorrow slumber
At the sight of the beauty that greets them, for the charm they
    have broken.

Hugh MacDiarmid
(1892-1978)

The Storm-Cock's Song

My song today is the storm-cock's song.
When the cold winds blow and the driving snow
Hides the tree-tops, only his song rings out
In the lulls in the storm. So let mine go !

On the topmost twig of a leafless ash
He sits bolt upright against the sky
Surveying the white fields and the leafless woods
And distant red in the East with his buoyant eye.

Surely he has little enough cause to sing
When even the hedgerow berries are already
     pulped by the frost
Or eaten by other birds – yet alone and aloft
To another hungry day his greeting is tossed.

Blessed are those who have songs to sing
When others are silent; poor song though it be,
Just a message to the silence that someone is still
Alive and glad, though on a naked tree.

What if it is only a few churning notes
Flung out in a loud and artless way?
His 'Will I do it? Do it I will !' is worth a lot
When the rest have nothing at all to say.

Storm cock: the country name for the song thrush.

Minnie Louise Haskins
(1875-1957)

The Gate of the Year

I said to the man who stood at the gate of the year:
    'Give me a light
    that I may tread safely into the unknown.'
And he replied:
    'Go out into the darkness
    and put your hand into the hand of God.
That shall be to you
    better than light,
    and safer than a known way.'

PART VI

I SAID TO MY SOUL, BE STILL

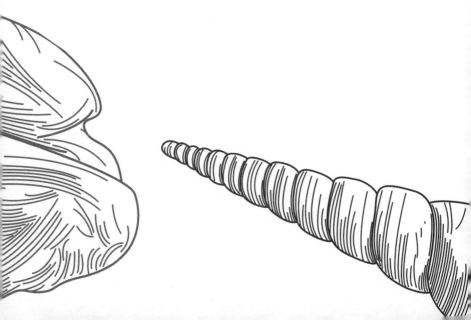

Anna McKenzie

Starting Over

And so we must begin to live again,
We of the damaged bodies
And assaulted minds.
Starting from scratch with the rubble of our lives
And picking up the dust
Of dreams once dreamt.

And we stand here, naked in our vulnerability,
Proud of starting over, fighting back,
But full of weak humility
At the awesomeness of the task.

We, without a future
Safe, defined, delivered,
Now salute you, God,
Knowing that nothing is safe,
Secure, inviolable here,
Except you,
And even you elude our minds at times.
And we hate you
As we love you,
And our anger is as strong
As our pain,
Our grief is deep as oceans,
And our need as great as mountains.

So, as we take our first few steps forward
Into the abyss of the future,
We would pray for

Courage to go places for the first time
And just be there.
Courage to become what we have
Not been before
And accept it,
And bravely to look deep
Within our souls to find
New ways.

We did not want it easy, God,
But we did not contemplate
That it would be quite this hard,
This long, this lonely.

So, if we are to be turned inside out,
And upside down,
With even our pockets shaken,
Just to check what's rattling
And left behind,
We pray that you will keep faith with us,
And we with you,
Holding our hands as we weep,
Giving us strength to continue,
And showing us beacons
Along the way
To becoming new.

We are not fighting you, God,
Even if it feels like it,
But we need your help and your company
As we struggle on,
Fighting back
And starting over.

E A Robinson
(1869-1935)

Credo

I cannot find my way: there is no star
In all the shrouded heavens anywhere;
And there is not a whisper in the air
Of any living voice but one so far
That I can hear it only as a bar
Of lost, imperial music, played when fair
And angel fingers wove, and unaware,
Dead leaves to garlands where no roses are.

No, there is not a glimmer, nor a call,
For one that welcomes, welcomes when he fears,
The black and awful chaos of the night: –
For through it all – above, beyond it all –
I know the far-sent message of the years,
I feel the coming glory of the Light.

R S Thomas
(1913-2000)

Via Negativa

Why no ! I never thought other than
That God is that great absence
In our lives, the empty silence
Within, the place where we go
Seeking, not in hope to
Arrive or find. He keeps the interstices
In our knowledge, the darkness
Between stars. His are the echoes
We follow, the footprints he has just
Left. We put our hands in
His side hoping to find
It warm. We look at people
And places as though he had looked
At them, too; but miss the reflection.

D H Lawrence
(1885-1930)

Shadows

And if tonight my soul may find her peace
in sleep, and sink in good oblivion,
and in the morning wake like a new-opened flower
then I have been dipped again in God, and new-created.

And if, as weeks go round, in the dark of the moon
my spirit darkens and goes out, and soft strange gloom
pervades my movements and my thoughts and words,
then I shall know that I am walking still
with God, we are close together now the moon's in shadow.

And if, as autumn deepens and darkens
I feel the pain of falling leaves and stems that break in storms
and trouble and dissolution and distress
and then the softness of deep shadows folding, folding
around my soul and spirit, around my lips
so sweet, like a swoon, or more like the drowse of a low, sad song
singing darker than the nightingale, on, on to the solstice
and the silence of short days, the silence of the year, the shadow,
then I shall know that my life is moving still
with the dark earth, and drenched
with the deep oblivion of earth's lapse and renewal.

And if, in the changing phases of man's life,
I fall in sickness and in misery
my wrists seem broken and my heart seems dead
and strength is gone, and my life
is only the leavings of a life:

and still, among it all, snatches of lovely oblivion, and snatches
    of renewal,
odd, wintry flowers upon the withered stem, yet new, strange flowers
such as my life has not brought forth before, new blossoms of me –

then I must know that still
I am in the hands of the unknown God,
he is breaking me down to his own oblivion
to send me forth on a new morning, a new man.

T S Eliot
(1888-1965)

I said to my soul, be still

I said to my soul, be still, and let the dark come upon you
Which shall be the darkness of God. As, in a theatre,
The lights are extinguished, for the scene to be changed
With a hollow rumble of wings, with a movement of darkness on darkness,
And we know that the hills and the trees, the distant panorama
And the bold imposing façade are all being rolled away –
Or as, when an underground train, in the tube, stops too long between stations
And the conversation rises and slowly fades into silence
And you see behind every face the mental emptiness deepen
Leaving only the growing terror of nothing to think about;
Or when, under ether, the mind is conscious but conscious of nothing –
I said to my soul, be still, and wait without hope
For hope would be hope for the wrong thing; wait without love,
For love would be love for the wrong thing; there is yet faith
But the faith and the love and the hope are all in the waiting.
Wait without thought, for you are not ready for thought:
So the darkness shall be the light, and the stillness the dancing.

Anonymous

Come, O Spirit of God

Come, O Spirit of God
And make within us your dwelling place and home.
May our darkness be dispelled by your light,
And our troubles calmed by your peace;
May all evils be redeemed by your love,
All pain transformed through the suffering of Christ,
And all dying glorified by his risen life.

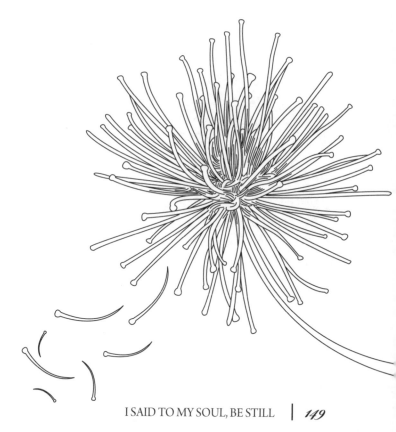

Anonymous

O Jesus, in your great loneliness

O Jesus, in your great loneliness
on the Mount of Olives, and in your Agony,
you did pray to the Heavenly Father for comfort.
You know that there are souls on earth who
are without support and without comforters,
pray send them an angel to give them joy.

Maria Luisa Spaziani
(*b* 1924)
tr. Philip Morre

Via Crucis [1]

Bronchitis tonight has made me
an oak-tree exhausted with snow.
Crucified to the earth with roots
of shivering and weakness,
I feel my heavy branches bow
under their load of a million crystals.

I knew a little boy once, far sicker
than I am: every breath was fought for,
he seemed a frigate blown inshore
onto the sandbanks of his bed, and still
his golden chatter was like orioles
high up in the blighted elm.

I'm thinking of him tonight,
though I know I'll soon be better.
I feel a little like that pietist
I saw in Bruges, in his otter-trim coat:
he was looking and looking at a Via Crucis,
trying to imagine the pain and the gall.

Perhaps there came to him too the notion
that it's not only the Christ of the icons,
on our long climb into darkness,
who goes before us, and for us.

---

[1] Stations of the Cross, a series of tableaux representing stages in the crucifixion of Christ.

Alexian Brothers
(adapted)

Prayer to Christ the Healer

In the comfort of your love,
I entrust to you, my Saviour,
the sickness that prevails upon me,
the anxieties that perplex me,
the fears that stifle me,
and the frustration of all the pain
that weaves about within me.
Lord, help me to see your peace in my turmoil,
your compassion in my sorrow,
your forgiveness in my weakness,
and your love in my need.
Touch me, O Lord, with your healing power and strength.

David Adam
(*b* 1936)

Circle me, Lord

Circle me, Lord.
Keep protection near
And danger afar.

Circle me, Lord.
Keep hope within.
Keep doubt without.

Circle me, Lord.
Keep light near
And darkness afar.

Circle me, Lord.
Keep peace within.
Keep evil out.

William Barclay
(1907-78)

Loving Father, help me to live one day at a time

Loving Father, help me to live one day at a time,
Not to be thinking of what might have been,
Not to be worrying about what may be.
Help me to accept the fact
That I cannot undo the past,
And I cannot foresee the future.
Help me to remember
That I will never be tried
Beyond what I can bear;
That a Father's hand will
Never cause his child a needless tear;
That I can never drift
Beyond your love and care.

King David

(*c* 1040-970BC)

The Lord is my shepherd

(*Psalm 23*)

The Lord is my shepherd; I shall not want.
He makes me lie down in green pastures;
He leads me beside still waters;
He restores my soul;
He leads me in the paths of righteousness for his name's sake.
Even though I walk through the valley of the shadow of death,
I fear no evil: for you are with me;
Your rod and your staff, they comfort me.
You prepare a table for me in the presence of my enemies;
You anoint my head with oil; my cup overflows.
Surely goodness and mercy shall follow me all the days of my life,
And I shall dwell in the house of the Lord for ever.

St Columba
(521-97)

Alone with none but you, my God

Alone with none but you, my God,
I journey on my way.
What need I fear when you are near,
O King of night and day?
More safe am I within your hand
than if a host should round me stand.

St Augustine of Hippo
(354-430)

Keep watch, dear Lord

Keep watch, dear Lord,
with those who wake, or watch, or weep this night,
and give your angels charge over those who sleep;
Tend those who are sick, O Lord Christ;
give rest to those who are weary,
bless those who are dying,
soothe those who are suffering,
pity those who are afflicted,
shield those who are joyous;
and all for your love's sake.

Dylan Thomas
(1914-53)

from

Under Milk Wood

At the doorway of Bethesda House, the Reverend Eli Jenkins
recites to Llareggub Hill his sunset poem:

Every morning when I wake,
Dear Lord, a little prayer I make,
O please to keep Thy lovely eye
On all poor creatures born to die.

And every evening at sun-down
I ask a blessing on the town,
For whether we last the night or no
I'm sure is always touch-and-go.

We are not wholly bad or good
Who live our lives under Milk Wood,
And Thou, I know, wilt be the first
To see our best side, not our worst.

O let us see another day !
Bless us all this night, I pray,
And to the sun we all will bow
And say, good-bye – but just for now !

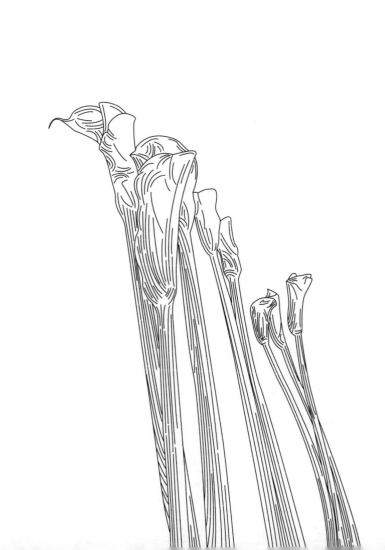

PART VII

LET EVENING COME

Welsh proverb

There are three things that only God knows:
the beginning of things;
the cause of things;
and the end of things.

George Herbert
(1593-1633)

from

The Flower

How fresh, O Lord, how sweet and clean
Are thy returns! ev'n as the flowers in spring;
      To which, besides their own demean,
The late-past frosts tributes of pleasure bring.
            Grief melts away
            Like snow in May,
      As if there were no such cold thing.

      Who would have thought my shrivel'd heart
Could have recover'd greennesse? It was gone
      Quite under ground; as flowers depart
To see their mother-root, when they have blown;
            Where they together
            All the hard weather,
      Dead to the world, keep house unknown.

      And now in age I bud again,
After so many deaths I live and write;
      I once more smell the dew and rain,
And relish versing: O my onely Light,
            It cannot be
            That I am he
      On whom Thy tempests fell all night.

Agatha Christie
(1890-1976)

Dartmoor

I shall not return again the way I came,
Back to the quiet country where the hills
Are purple in the evenings, and the tors
Are grey and quiet, and the tall standing stones
Lead out across the moorland till they end
At water's edge.
It is too gentle, all that land,
It will bring back
Such quiet dear remembered things,
There, where the longstone lifts its lonely head,
Gaunt, grey, forbidding,
Ageless, however worn away;
There, even, grows the heather…
Tender, kind,
The little streams are busy in the valleys,
The rivers meet by the grey Druid bridge,
So quiet,
So quiet,
Not as death is quiet, but as life can be quiet
When it is sweet.

Willa Cather
(1873-1947)

Going Home

(Burlington Route)

How smoothly the train runs beyond the Missouri;
Even in my sleep I know when I have crossed the river.
The wheels turn as if they were glad to go;
The sharp curves and windings left behind,
The roadway wide open,
(The crooked straight
And the rough places plain.)[1]

They run smoothly, they run softly, too.
There is not noise enough to trouble the lightest sleeper.
Nor jolting to wake the weary-hearted.
I open my window and let the air blow in,
The air of morning,
That smells of grass and earth –
Earth, the grain-giver.

How smoothly the trains run beyond the Missouri;
Even in my sleep I know when I have crossed the river.
The wheels turn as if they were glad to go;
  They run like running water,
  Like Youth, running away...

---

[1] 'The crooked shall be made straight, and the rough places plain: and the glory of the Lord shall be revealed' – Isaiah 40:4–5.

They spin bright along the bright rails,
Singing and humming,
Singing and humming,
They run remembering,
They run rejoicing,
As if they, too, were going home.

Charles Causley
(1917-2003)

Eden Rock

They are waiting for me somewhere beyond Eden Rock:
My father, twenty-five, in the same suit
Of Genuine Irish Tweed, his terrier Jack
Still two years old and trembling at his feet.

My mother, twenty-three, in a sprigged dress
Drawn at the waist, ribbon in her straw hat,
Has spread the stiff white cloth over the grass.
Her hair, the colour of wheat, takes on the light.

She pours tea from a Thermos, the milk straight
From an old H.P. sauce bottle, a screw
Of paper for a cork; slowly sets out
The same three plates, the tin cups painted blue.

The sky whitens as if lit by three suns.
My mother shades her eyes and looks my way
Over the drifted stream. My father spins
A stone along the water. Leisurely,

They beckon to me from the other bank.
I hear them call, ' See where the stream-path is !
Crossing is not as hard as you might think.'

I had not thought that it would be like this.

Rudyard Kipling
(1865-1936)

The Way through the Woods

They shut the road through the woods
Seventy years ago.
Weather and rain have undone it again,
And now you would never know
There was once a road through the woods
Before they planted the trees.
It is underneath the coppice and heath,
And the thin anemones.
Only the keeper sees
That, where the ring-dove broods,
And the badgers roll at ease,
There was once a road through the woods.

Yet, if you enter the woods
Of a summer evening late,
When the night-air cools on the trout-
ringed pools
Where the otter whistles his mate,
(They fear not men in the woods,
Because they see so few.)
You will hear the beat of a horse's feet,
And the swish of a skirt in the dew,
Steadily cantering through
The misty solitudes,
As though they perfectly knew
The old lost road through the woods.
But there is no road through the woods.

John Donne
(1572-1631)

Thou hast made me, And shall thy worke decay?

Thou hast made me, And shall thy worke decay?
Repaire me now, for now mine end doth haste,
I runne to death, and death meets me as fast,
And all my pleasures are like yesterday;
I dare not move my dimme eyes any way,
Despaire behind, and death before doth cast
Such terrour, and my feeble flesh doth waste
By sinne in it, which it t'wards hell doth weigh;
Onely thou art above, and when towards thee
By thy leave I can looke, I rise againe;
But our old subtle foe so tempteth me,
That not one houre my selfe I can sustaine;
Thy Grace may wing me to prevent his art,   [*frustrate*
And thou like Adamant draw mine iron heart.   [*a magnet*

John Keats
(1795-1821)

When I have fears that I may cease to be

When I have fears that I may cease to be
    Before my pen has glean'd my teeming brain,
Before high piled books, in charact'ry,   [*printed words*
    Hold like rich garners the full-ripen'd grain;   [*granaries*
When I behold, upon the night's starr'd face,
    Huge cloudy symbols of a high romance,
And think that I may never live to trace
    Their shadows, with the magic hand of chance;
And when I feel, fair creature of an hour!
    That I shall never look upon thee more,
Never have relish in the faery power
    Of unreflecting love! – then on the shore
Of the wide world I stand alone, and think
Till Love and Fame to nothingness do sink.

Ivor Gurney
(1890-1937)

The songs I had

The songs I had are withered
Or vanished clean,
Yet there are bright tracks
Where I have been,

And there grow flowers
For others' delight.
Think well, O singer,
Soon comes night.

Molly Holden
(1927-81)

The seed the hornbeam casts

The seed the hornbeam casts
will not be seen by me
to elevate from sapling
into a graceful tree.

But though I leave the scene,
as leave the scene I must,
I too have cast my seedlings
into the human dust.

Helen Dunmore
(*b* 1952)

I should like to be buried in a summer forest

I should like to be buried in a summer forest
where people go in July,
only a bus ride from the city,

I should like them to walk over me
not noticing anything but sunlight
and patches of wild strawberries –

Here! Look under the leaves!
I should like the child who is slowest
to end up picking the most,

and the big kids will show the little
the only way to grasp the nettle
and pick it so it doesn't sting.

I should like home-time to come
so late the bus has its lights on
and a cloud of moths hangs in their beam,

and when they are all gone
I should like to be buried in a summer forest
where the dark steps
blindfold, on cat foot-pads,
with the dawn almost touching it.

Jane Kenyon
(1947-95)

Let Evening Come

Let the light of late afternoon
shine through chinks in the barn, moving
up the bales as the sun moves down.

Let the cricket take up chafing
as a woman takes up her needles
and her yarn. Let evening come.

Let dew collect on the hoe abandoned
in long grass. Let the stars appear
and the moon disclose her silver horn.

Let the fox go back to its sandy den.
Let the wind die down. Let the shed
go black inside. Let evening come.

To the bottle in the ditch, to the scoop
in the oats, to air in the lung
let evening come.

Let it come, as it will, and don't
be afraid. God does not leave us
comfortless, so let evening come.

Pär Lagerkvist
(1891-1974)
tr. W H Auden & Leif Sjöberg

Everything is so strangely removed today

Everything is so strangely removed today,
so far far away.
Within the clouds is heard the beating of the wings
of birds, far far away.

Clear as a bell of silver and glass,
far far away,
a bird's voice resounds brittle as glass
in a sky far far away.

Alone in the light of evening I hearken.
How the days begin to shorten.
Autumn has come. Soon my day will grow dim.
I hear wings so far far away.

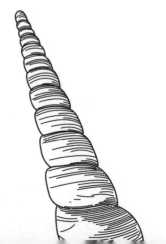

Sasha Moorsom
(1931-93)

The Company of the Birds

Ah the company of the birds
I loved and cherished on earth
Now, freed of flesh we fly
Together, a flock of beating wings,
I am as light, as feathery,
As gone from gravity we soar
In endless circles.

John G Magee
(1922-1941)

High Flight

Oh! I have slipped the surly bonds of Earth
And danced the skies on laughter-silvered wings;
Sunward I've climbed, and joined the tumbling mirth
Of sun-split clouds, and done a hundred things
You have not dreamed of – wheeled and soared and swung
High in the sunlit silence. Hov'ring there,
I've chased the shouting wind along, and flung
My eager craft through footless halls of air …

Up, up the long, delirious, burning blue
I've topped the windswept heights with easy grace
Where never lark nor ever eagle flew –
And, while with silent lifting mind I've trod
The high untrespassed sanctity of space,
Put out my hand, and touched the face of God.

W E Henley
(1849-1903)

I. M. Margaritae Sorori [1]

A late lark twitters from the quiet skies;
And from the west,
Where the sun, his day's work ended,
Lingers as in content
There falls on the old, gray city
An influence luminous and serene,
A shining peace.

The smoke ascends
In a rosy-and-golden haze. The spires
Shine, and are changed. In the valley
Shadows rise. The lark sings on. The sun,
Closing his benediction,
Sinks, and the darkening air
Thrills with a sense of the triumphing night –
Night with her train of stars
And her great gift of sleep.

So be my passing!
My task accomplished and the long day done,
My wages taken, and in my heart
Some late lark singing,
Let me be gathered to the quiet west,
The sundown splendid and serene,
Death.

---

[1] 'In Memory of [my] Sister Margaret'.

Thomas Campion
(1567-1620)

Never weather-beaten Saile

Never weather-beaten Saile more willing bent to shore,
Never tyred Pilgrim's limbs affected slumber more,   *[longed for*
Than my wearied spright now longs to flye out of my   *[spirit*
    troubled brest:
O come quickly, sweetest Lord, and take my soule to rest.

Ever-blooming are the joys of Heav'ns high paradice,
Cold age deafes not there our eares, nor vapour dims our eyes;
Glory there the Sun outshines, whose beames the blessèd
    onely see:
O come quickly, glorious Lord, and raise my spright to thee.

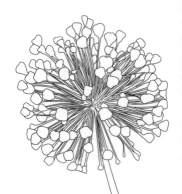

Amelia Josephine Burr
(1878-1968)

A Song of Living

Because I have loved life, I shall have no sorrow to die.
I have sent up my gladness on wings, to be lost in the blue of the sky.
I have run and leaped with the rain, I have taken the wind to my breast.
My cheek like a drowsy child to the face of the earth I have pressed.
Because I have loved life, I shall have no sorrow to die.

I have kissed young Love on the lips, I have heard his song to the end.
I have struck my hand like a seal in the loyal hand of a friend.
I have known the peace of heaven, the comfort of work done well.
I have longed for death in the darkness and risen alive out of hell.
Because I have loved life, I shall have no sorrow to die.

I give a share of my soul to the world, when and where my course is run.
I know that another shall finish the task I surely must leave undone.
I know that no flower, nor flint was in vain on the path I once did travel.
But, I sipped nectar and wine when all of life's mysteries did slowly unravel.
Because I have loved life, I shall have no sorrow to die.

Christina Rossetti
(1830-94)

Remember

Remember me when I am gone away,
    Gone far away into the silent land;
When you can no more hold me by the hand,
    Nor I half turn to go, yet turning stay.
Remember me when no more day by day
    You tell me of our future that you plann'd:
    Only remember me; you understand
It will be late to counsel then or pray.
Yet if you should forget me for a while
    And afterwards remember, do not grieve:
    For if the darkness and corruption leave
    A vestige of the thoughts that once I had,
Better by far you should forget and smile
    Than that you should remember and be sad.

Henry Scott Holland
(1847-1918)

Death is nothing at all

Death is nothing at all:
I have only slipped away into the next room.
I am I, and you are you;
Whatever we were to each other, we are still.

Speak of me in the easy way you always used:
Wear no air of solemnity or sorrow;
Laugh as we always laughed at the little jokes we enjoyed together;
Play, smile, think of me, pray for me.

What is this death but a negligible accident?
Why should I be out of mind because I am out of sight?
I am but waiting for you, somewhere very near, just around the corner.
All is well.

Christina Rossetti
(1830-94)

Time Flies

Time flies, hope flags, life plies a wearied wing;
 Death following hard on life gains ground apace;
 Faith runs with each and rears an eager face,
Outruns the rest, makes light of everything,
Spurns earth, and still finds breath to pray and sing;
 While love ahead of all uplifts his praise,
 Still asks for grace and still gives thanks for grace,
Content with all day brings and night will bring.
Life wanes; and when love folds his wings above
 Tired hope, and less we feel his conscious pulse,
  Let us go fall asleep, dear friend, in peace:
  A little while, and age and sorrow cease;
 A little while, life reborn annuls
Loss and decay and death, and all is love.

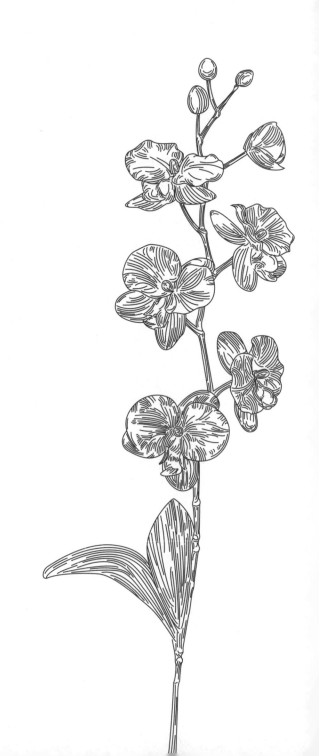

SUGGESTED READING

Albery, Nicholas, *Poem for the Day One* (Chatto & Windus, 1994) – a wide-ranging introductory anthology of well-known and little-known poems, one for each day of the year, each with fascinating commentary on the poem or the poet's life. Also, *Poem for the Day Two* (Chatto & Windus, 2005), by the same editor.

Astley, **Neil**, ed., *Staying Alive: Real poems for unreal times* (Bloodaxe Books, 2002) – 500 life-affirming poems 'helping us stay alive to the world and true to ourselves'. There are two further sequels: *Being Alive* (Bloodaxe Books, 2004) and *Being Human* (Bloodaxe Books, 2011), both by the same editor.

Barber, **Laura**, ed., *Poems for Life* (Penguin Books, 2007) – poems for all the stages of life, from infancy and adolescence to working, family life, ageing, approaching death and bereavement.

Barclay, **William**, *Prayers for Help and Healing* (Augsburg Fortress, 1995) – prayers for sickness, pain and anxiety in hospital, and for those who care for the sick.

Batchelor, **Mary**, *The Lion Christian Poetry Collection* (Lion Publishing, 1995) – an exhaustive (almost 600-page) anthology of poems spanning 1000 years, including a high proportion of rewarding lesser-known and modern poets not to be encountered in conventional anthologies.

Colby, Jane, ed., *Young Hearts: Inspirational poetry by children and young people with ME* (The Young ME Sufferers Trust, Ingatestone, 2004) – movingly honest poems that express every aspect of living with this illness.

Darling, Julia and **Cynthia Fuller**, *The Poetry Cure* (Bloodaxe Books, 2005) – poems that help understand illness, doctors, hospitals, loss and bereavement.

Enright, D J, *The Faber Book of Fevers and Frets* (Faber & Faber, 1989) – an entertaining anthology of poems and prose about (mostly non-fatal) conditions such as phobias, manias, love sickness and madness.

Ewart, Gavin, *The Penguin Book of Light Verse* (Penguin Books, 1980) – one of the most entertaining collections of comic, curious and cheerful verse for grown-up children.

Forbes, Peter, ed., *We Have Come Through: 100 poems celebrating courage in overcoming depression and trauma* (Bloodaxe Books, 2003).

Fox, John, *Poetic Medicine: The Healing Art of Poem-Making* (Jeremy P Tarcher/Putnam, 1999) – a practical workbook by the leading American 'poetry therapist' about how to draw on the healing force of creative writing about one's experience of illness.

Goodwin, Daisy, ed., *101 Poems That Could Save your Life: An anthology of emotional first aid* (HarperCollins, 1999) – poems for crises, the blues, bad luck, loss and other bad stuff.

Gross, John, *The Oxford Book of Comic Verse* (Oxford University Press, 1995) – like Gavin Ewart's *Penguin Book of Light Verse* only different.

Jamison, Kay Redfield, *An Unquiet Mind: A memoir of moods and madness* (Picador, 1997) – a courageous and candid prose memoir of suffering from bipolar disorder by the foremost scholar of the illness.

Jones, Griff Rhys, ed., *The Nation's Favourite Poems* (BBC Books, 1996) – all the best-loved poems that everybody can recite or half-remember some lines from.

Keegan, Paul, ed., *New Penguin Book of English Verse* (Penguin Books, 2004) – an exceptionally varied collection of the best of English poetry.

McAinsh, Beverley, ed., with Introduction by Mark Tully, *Something Understood* (Hodder & Stoughton, 2002) – a rewarding anthology of poems and prose to aid understanding of love and friendship, youth and age, aspiration, yearning for God, consolation in pain and trouble, and the spiritual trajectory of our lives.

Nash, Ogden, ed. Anthony Burgess, *Candy is Dandy: The best of Ogden Nash* (Carlton Books, 1994) – irresistible lyrics by the funniest versifier of the twentieth century.

O'Malley, William J, ed., *Daily Prayers for Busy People* (St Mary's Press, 1990) – a stimulating cycle of daily devotions made up of poems, extracts from the Bible and other works of literature, as well as nourishing original prayers written by the editor. There is a second volume, *More Daily Prayers for Busy People* (2003), by the same editor.

Patten, Brian, *The Puffin Book of Utterly Brilliant Poetry* (Puffin, 1999) – a delightful, colourfully illustrated collection of silly verse for children young and old.

Reid, Christopher, *Sounds Good: 101 poems to be heard* (Faber & Faber, 1998) – mellifluous poems that revel in the musical qualities of verse.

Rosen, Kim, *Saved by a Poem: The transformative power of words* (Hay House, 2009) – an engrossing and lucid exploration of the ways in which poetry can bring the reader pleasure, healing and change. With accompanying CD of the poems that are discussed in detail.

Smith, Ken and **Matthew Sweeney**, eds., *Beyond Bedlam: Poems written out of mental distress* (Anvil Press, 1997) – historical and present-day verse that is testament to the value of the imagination in transcending the distress of mental illness.

ACKNOWLEDGEMENTS

I am deeply indebted to many people, too numerous to name, for their creative suggestions and moral support in the compilation of this book. Above all I am grateful to my wife, Monica, for her good sense and encouragement throughout its compilation. To Sylvia Scott, with her long experience of illness first as a nurse and now courageously enduring severe illness herself, I am extremely grateful for so freely giving me the benefit of her wide knowledge and love of poetry. Elizabeth Kerr encouraged me by immediately responding to the concept of poetic consolation during illness and, with her sister Margaret, helping me sift my shortlist from the viewpoint of the prospective reader. Margaret Forey generously helped me shape my Introduction and vetted my poets' biographies during a low phase of my illness. Following several articles I wrote in the press on the subject of 'the poetry of consolation', I was inundated with letters and emails from readers about their own therapeutic experience of reading poetry and suggesting particular poems, prayers, and sometimes whole collections that most helped them cope with their illnesses. To the hundreds of people who took the trouble to write to me I am enormously grateful, though it would be impractical to list more than those whose suggestions finally made it into this book: Naomi Ackroyd, William Allsop, Ann Baer, Sue Barrett, David Bartlett, Andrew Bennerton, Vivien Bradley, Catherine Brady, Michael Burr, Diane Calabrese, Sian Cardell, Anna Corrigan, Miles Crittendon, Margaret Forey, Anna Gale, David Hart, Joan Henwood, Sr Katherine Holmström, Anthony Imms, Alice Jupp, C A M Keefe, Dr Jean Kennedy, David Lees, Fr Simon Leakey, Alan

Macknight, Trish Mitchell, Philip Morre, Ralph Ockendon, Patrick O'Connor, Jennifer Ormerod, Ruth Pike, Liam Parker, Sr Teresa Reilly, Martin Richards, Ann Robertson, Sylvia Scott, Philippa di Stephano, Dorothy Tipper, the Tymes Trust, Anne Wawszczyk, Mary Wolstenholme, Sr Marguerite Wong and John Woodard.

I am especially grateful to the majority of poets and publishers I approached who have generously allowed their work to appear here free of charge or for a nominal fee, and I acknowledge in the following list the permission granted by all those who allowed me to reprint their copyright material. Those who have proved unreachable despite my best efforts I would ask to contact me so that amends can be made in a future edition.

Please note that all the following poems are copyright-protected against unauthorised copying whether in print, on the internet, broadcast or in any other medium:

Dannie Abse, 'A Wall' from *New and Collected Poems* (Hutchinson, 2003): by permission of Random House Group Ltd.

David Adam, 'Circle me, Lord' from *The Edge of Glory: Prayers in the Celtic tradition* (SPCK, 2011): by permission of SPCK Publishing.

Alexian Brothers, 'Prayer to Christ the Healer': by kind permission of Dr Joseph Locke and the Alexian Brothers of America.

W H Auden, extract from 'In memory of W B Yeats' from *Collected Poems*, copyright © The Estate of W H Auden 1976, 1991. All rights reserved. Used by permission of the Wylie Agency (UK). US copyright 1940 and renewed 1968 by W H Auden, from *Collected Poems of W H Auden*. Used by permission of Doubleday, a Division of Random House, Inc.

William Barclay, 'Loving Father, help me to live one day at a time' from *Prayers for Help and Healing* (1968): by permission of HarperCollins Publishers Ltd © 1968 William Barclay.

Wendell Berry, 'The Peace of Wild Things', copyright © 1998 by Wendell Berry from *The Selected Poems of Wendell Berry* (1999): by permission of Counterpoint Press.

Laurence Binyon, 'The Burning of the Leaves' from *Selected Poems* (2009): by permission of the Society of Authors as the Literary Representative of the Estate of Laurence Binyon..

Elizabeth Bishop, 'I am in need of music' ('Sonnet', 1928) from *The Complete Poems 1927-1979* (2004). Copyright © 1979, 1983 by Alice Helen Methfessel. Reprinted by permission of Farrar, Straus and Giroux, LLC.

Robert Bly, translation of Rainer Maria Rilke's 'Sunset' from *Selected Poems of Rainer Maria Rilke: a translation from the German and commentary by Robert Bly* (1981). Copyright © 1981 by Robert Bly. Reprinted by permission of HarperCollins Publishers.

Sharon Brogan, 'Fibromyalgia': by kind permission of the author.

Willa Cather, 'Going Home' from *April Twilights* by Willa Cather, copyright © 1923 by Willa Cather and renewed 1951 by the Executors of the Estate of Willa Cather. Used by permission of Alfred A Knopf, a division of Random House, Inc.

Charles Causley, 'Eden Rock' from *Collected Poems* (Picador 2000): by permission of David Higham Associates.

Agatha Christie, 'Dartmoor' from *Poems* (1973) © 2011 by Agatha Christie Limited (a Chorion company). All rights reserved.

Oscar Hammerstein, You'll Never Walk Alone' copyright © 1945 by Richard Rodgers and Oscar Hammerstein II. Copyright renewed. International copyright secured. All rights reserved. Used by permission of Williamson Music, a division of Rodgers & Hammerstein: an Imagem company.

Minnie Louise Haskins, 'The Gate of the Year' © Minnie Louise Haskins, 1908: by permission of Sheil Land Associates Ltd.

Molly Holden, 'Proverb' and 'The seed the hornbeam casts' from *Selected Poems* (1987): by kind permission of Gerard Holden and Nicola Carpenter.

Catie Jenkins (now Cate Allison), 'Please Don't' first published in *Young Hearts: Inspirational poetry by children and young people with ME* (The Young ME Sufferers Trust, 2004): by kind permission of the author.

Elizabeth Jennings, 'Pain' from 'Sequence in Hospital' in *New Collected Poems* (Carcanet Press, 2002): by permission of David Higham Associates.

Jane Kenyon, 'Now Where?' and 'Let Evening Come' from *Collected Poems* (2005). Copyright © 2005 by the Estate of Jane Kenyon. Reprinted with the permission of The Permissions Company, Inc., on behalf of Graywolf Press, Minneapolis, Minnesota (www.graywolfpress.org).

James Kirkup, 'There is a new morning' from 'Six Poems' in *An Extended Breath: Collected Longer Poems and Sequences* (Poetry Salzburg, formerly University of Salzburg Press, 1996): by permission of Poetry Salzburg.

Pär Lagerkvist, 'Everything is so strangely removed today' from *Evening Land* (1997) by Pär Lagerkvist, translated by W H Auden

Young, ed. Sophie Young (Carcanet Press, 1994): by kind permission of the publisher.

Philip Morre, translation of 'Via Crucis' by Maria Luisa Spaziani, copyright © Arnoldo Mondadori Editore, Milano: by kind permission of the author, translator and Arnoldo Mondadori Editore.

John O'Donohue, 'For a Friend, on the Arrival of Illness' from *Benedictus: A Book of Blessings* (2007) published in the UK by Bantam Press, reprinted by permission of The Random House Group Ltd. In the USA the poem is published in *To Bless the Space Between Us: A Book of Blessings* (2008) copyright © 2008 by John O'Donohue. Reprinted by permission of Doubleday, a division of Random House, Inc.

William J O'Malley, 'Lord, I am tangled in a net of confusion and doubts' from *Daily Prayers for Busy People* (1990), and 'By the Rivers of Babylon' from *More Daily Prayers for Busy People* (2003): by permission of Liguori Publications.

Mary Oliver, 'Wild Geese' from *Dream Work* (1994). Copyright © 1986 by Mary Oliver. Used by permission of Grove/Atlantic, Inc.

Ruth Pitter, 'Cure me with quietness' from *Collected Poems* (Enitharmon Press, 1996): by kind permission of the publisher.

Kathleen Raine, 'April's new apple buds' from *The Collected Poems of Kathleen Raine* (Golgonooza Press, 2000): copyright the Literary Estate of Kathleen Raine, reprinted by kind permission.

A Mary F Robinson, 'Neurasthenia' from Collected Poems (A & C Black, 1902): by permission of the publisher.

Thomas. Reprinted by permission of David Higham Associates and New Directions Publishing Corp; and 'Every morning when I wake' from *Under Milk Wood* (2000), reprinted by permission of David Higham Associates and New Directions Publishing Corp.

R S Thomas, 'Via Negativa' from *Collected Poems* (Phoenix, 2000): by permission of Orion Publishing.

Tomas Tranströmer, 'Tracks', translated by Robin Fulton, from *New Collected Poems* (Bloodaxe Books, 2000): by kind permission of the publisher.

Derek Walcott, 'Love after Love' from *Collected Poems 1948-1984* (1992). Copyright © 1986 by Derek Walcott. Reprinted by permission of Farrar, Straus, and Giroux, LLC and Faber & Faber Ltd.

Arthur Waley, translations of Po Chu-ï, 'Winter Night' and 'Being Visited by a Friend during illness' from *Translations from the Chinese* (1946): by permission of The Arthur Waley Estate.

Jan Williams, 'Loss' first published in *InterAction* (no. 54, November 2005), the journal of Action for ME: by kind permission of the author.

LIVES OF THE POETS

DANNIE ABSE (b1923) was born in Cardiff, Wales, and has worked mainly as a hospital doctor while also writing poetry, plays, memoirs and other books. His genial, observant poems often reflect his Welshness and his love of music, while many others arise from his medical experience and reveal his compassionate response to suffering.

DAVID ADAM (b1936) was born in Alnwick, Northumberland, and left school at fifteen to work as a miner. After three years he trained for the ministry and served as vicar of Danby in Yorkshire for over twenty years, where he began writing prayers in the Celtic tradition. He later became vicar of the Holy Island of Lindisfarne, where he now lives in retirement.

The ALEXIAN BROTHERS are a lay Catholic order who dedicate themselves to living and working in the community in various branches of the healing ministries. The Order was inspired by the fourth-century Saint Alexius, who came from a wealthy Roman family but lived anonymously as a beggar, sharing his alms with the poor and serving for many years in a hospital in Edessa, Syria (now in Turkey).

MATTHEW ARNOLD (1822-88) was a poet and cultural critic who worked as a schools inspector (he was the son of Thomas Arnold, the famous headmaster of Rugby School). His best-known poem is 'Dover Beach', a lament for the decline of religious belief and an endorsement of love as its only true successor. The quoted lines are from 'Thyrsis', written in commemoration of his close friend the poet Arthur Hugh Clough.

St Augustine of Hippo (354-430) – not to be confused with St Augustine the first Archbishop of Canterbury – lived and died in Algeria and was one of the early Church Fathers, the most important Christian thinker after St Paul. His principal works are *The City of God* and *Confessions*, and his particular synthesis of Christian, Roman and Platonic thought defined the terms of much subsequent Christian theology.

William Barclay (1907-78), a Church of Scotland minister and Professor of Divinity at the University of Glasgow, was an influential writer who dedicated his life to explaining the Bible to the general reader. He had an outstanding gift for communicating the meaning of Scripture in a down-to-earth and enthusiastic manner, and his *Daily Bible Study* commentaries have been bestsellers since they were first published.

Wendell Berry (*b* 1934) grew up on a farm in Henry County, Kentucky, where he continues to live and work. His quiet, meditative poetry often turns on themes of the power of natural cycles, family responsibility, and the importance of community. He is a vigorous campaigner on environmental and political issues, seeing in the natural world models for human organisation.

Laurence Binyon (1869-1943), son of an Anglican vicar of Quaker ancestry, was a poet, playwright and Oriental art historian, for twenty years Keeper of Oriental Prints and Drawings at the British Museum. His best-known poem was 'For the Fallen', with its famous line 'They shall grow not old, as we that are left grow old', which was engraved on First World War memorials throughout the world.

ELIZABETH BISHOP (1911-79) was one of the most important American poets of the twentieth century, revered for her vivid and precise evocations of scene and circumstance and her empathy for her fellow beings, animal as well as human. As a child she suffered severely from asthma and eczema, and in later life was often anxious, depressed and dependent on alcohol. She wrote 'I am in need of music' at the age of seventeen when she was at boarding school.

WILLIAM BLAKE (1757-1827) was the earliest and most original of the Romantic poets, the visionary author and illustrator of works such as *Songs of Innocence* and *Experience and Daughters of Albion*. He was frequently visited by angels and other visions, and was generally considered harmlessly mad. His best-known lines have been set as the hymn 'Jerusalem', which has become almost a second English national anthem.

ROBERT BRIDGES (1844-1930) was a wealthy, cultured dilettante who spent his life in the study and practice of poetry, music, language, hymnology, and other aesthetic interests. He was never a very popular poet, though he did serve as Poet Laureate from 1913 until his death, and has since fallen into almost complete obscurity. He is remembered for the hymn translation 'All my hope on God is founded' and a handful of poems, of which 'London Snow' may be the best known.

SHARON BROGAN (*b* 1948) lives in western Montana, USA, and was Program Director of a community mental health centre when she fell ill with fibromyalgia and ME. Her poetry has appeared in various publications and online venues, though she now rarely seeks publication. She is also active, when illness allows, as an amateur photographer and blogger, a medium she considers an art form distinct in itself.

ROBERT BROWNING (1812-89) was one of the foremost poets of the Victorian era, best known for his lifelong romance with the invalid poet Elizabeth Barrett Browning and for his poems 'The Pied Piper of Hamelin' and 'How They Brought the Good News from Ghent to Aix'. When Elizabeth's father forbade her marriage to Robert, the young couple eloped to Italy, where they lived until her death in 1861.

JOHN BUNYAN (1628-88) was a Baptist writer and preacher, and author of *The Pilgrim's Progress*, the most influential and widely translated religious book in English apart from the Bible. Written while Bunyan was in prison for his unorthodox preaching, the book is an allegory describing the obstacles and temptations met by the pilgrim Christian on his way from the City of Destruction to the Celestial City.

AMELIA JOSEPHINE BURR (1878-1968) was an American poet about whom little is known, save that she was born in New York, married a clergyman in New Jersey, and during the First World War worked for the Red Cross. She published several novels, verse collections and poetry anthologies.

THOMAS CAMPION (1567-1620) was a composer, poet, theorist and physician, and one of the outstanding songwriters of the English lutenist school of the late sixteenth century. As a songwriter he was second only to John Dowland, and his lyrics were among the finest of the age. After his death, however, his songs and lyrics fell into complete obscurity and remained unrecovered until 1889, when a complete edition was published.

WILLA CATHER (1873-1947) was one of the most important American novelists of the early twentieth century, who chronicled frontier life in the American Great Plains in novels such as *My Antonia*, and *One of Ours*, for which she won the Pulitzer Prize in 1922. Critics praised her for writing about ordinary people in plain-spoken language, and for her subtle characterisation of human relationships under changing conditions.

CHARLES CAUSLEY (1917-2003) was one of the most popular poets of the twentieth century. He was born, lived (apart from war service) and died in Launceston, Cornwall, where he was a primary school teacher. In many of his poems there is a deceptive simplicity that makes them easy for readers of all ages to understand, though it is his children's verse that is best known today, poems such as 'Timothy Winters' and 'I Saw a Jolly Hunter'.

JANE CAVE (c1754-1813) is completely unknown apart from what can be inferred from her published poems, which suggest that she may have been Welsh, and may have worked as a servant or teacher.

AGATHA CHRISTIE (1890-1976) is the most famous of English crime writers, in particular for her novels featuring Hercule Poirot and Miss

Marple. During the First and Second World Wars she worked in hospital pharmacies, where she gained the extensive knowledge of poisons used in many of her books. She also wrote three volumes of poetry, one of them a series of poems and stories expressing her strong religious belief.

JOHN CLARE (1793-1864) has been called 'the greatest labouring-class poet England has ever produced', for his powerful writing about nature, rural childhood, and the instability caused by his mental illness. Although his poetry was favourably received by the London literary elite, he never felt valued, and fell prey to depression and alcohol, which hastened his mental decline. From 1841 until his death he was confined to a lunatic asylum.

ST COLUMBA (in Gaelic, Colum Cille, 521-97) was an Irish missionary monk who is credited with introducing Christianity to the Picts (Scots) and founded a monastery on the island of Iona. He went on to establish churches all over Scotland, and was the author of several hymns.

FRANCES CORNFORD (1886-1960) was a member of the illustrious Darwin–Wedgwood family, daughter of the botanist Francis Darwin and granddaughter of Charles Darwin, proponent of the theory of evolution. Like him she suffered all her life from long episodes of severe depression, which no doubt caused the feeling of marginalisation from the mainstream of life that forms a constant theme in her poetry.

DINAH MARIA MULOCK CRAIK (1826-87), daughter of an unconventional Nonconformist pastor, was one of the most popular

English women novelists of her day, author of the moralistic *John Halifax, Gentleman* (1856) and *A Life for a Life* (1859), from which the quoted extract is taken. Originally written in prose, these lines are the only writing for which she is now remembered.

E E CUMMINGS (1894-1962), the son of a Harvard professor and Unitarian minister, is famous for (at first) lower-case-ing his name and for his eccentric punctuation and sentence structure, intended to extend the functional expressiveness of language. His inventive verbal and visual experiments, jokiness and satire, along with his spiritual seriousness and often sentimental tenderness, made him one of the most popular American poets of the twentieth century.

KING DAVID (*c* 1040-970BC) was the second King of Israel and founder of the dynasty from which Jesus Christ was descended. An acclaimed warrior, musician and poet, he is credited with composing much of the biblical Book of Psalms. As a youth he was famed for his bravery and skill with the harp, with which he soothed King Saul's madness, and in battle against the Philistines he triumphed in single combat with the giant Goliath armed only with a shepherd's sling.

EMILY DICKINSON (1830-86), arguably the greatest of American poets, spent her adult life in almost total seclusion. She rarely allowed publication of her intense, enigmatic lyrics, and after her death her 1,789 poems were discovered hidden away in small hand-sewn booklets; it took many decades for their originality and psychological insight to be fully recognised. Her punctuation is notoriously puzzling: the dashes are clearly not intended as long pauses but are indeterminate punctuation which can only be interpreted by reading aloud.

JOHN DONNE (1572-1631), the most important of the Metaphysical Poets, was born into a wealthy Catholic family but converted to the Anglican church and rose to become Dean of St Paul's Cathedral, London. His poetry is characterised by its vibrancy, passion, intellectual complexity and elegant word-play, and though his early love poems are best known he also wrote memorable religious verse and sermons.

HELEN DUNMORE (b 1952) is a poet, novelist, critic, children's writer and teacher of creative writing in universities, schools, hospitals and prisons. She is best known for her novels, such as *The Siege* and *The Betrayal*, both of which draw on her lifelong love of Russian history, culture and literature. As in all her writings, these display her rare gift for conjuring up for the reader the physical and psychical sensations of being truly present in the stories she tells.

T S ELIOT (1888-1965), probably the most influential poet of the twentieth century, was born in America but lived and was buried in England. His poems 'The Love Song of J Alfred Prufrock' and *The Waste Land* changed the course of British and American poetry, but ironically outside the literary world he is best known as the writer who inspired the musical *Cats*, based on the comic-verse sequence *Old Possum's Book of Practical Cats*. The lines of 'I said to my soul' come from 'East Coker' in *Four Quartets*.

JOHN FLETCHER (1579-1625) was one of the most prolific Jacobean playwrights, the author of more than sixty plays either alone or in collaboration with other playwrights, among them Francis Beaumont and Shakespeare. He is thought to have died of the plague.

Victoria Flute (b1978) was born in Suffolk and fell ill with ME when she was thirteen. She struggled to complete school and was virtually bedbound for many years. She wrote 'On Hold' for the Tymes [The Young ME Sufferers] Trust anthology *Young Hearts: Inspirational poetry by children and young people with ME* (2004), and though she is still 'on hold', she is moving towards the front of the queue.

Robert Frost (1874-1963), 'the voice of New England', was a teacher and farmer before first publishing his poetry, which is characterised by the authentic rhythms of American vernacular speech. He suffered many family tragedies in his life, in addition to the congenital depression he fought against by undertaking practical work such as that described in one of his best-known poems, 'Mending Wall'.

Sheila Gay lives in Devon, England, where she is a Church of England Lay Reader. Family and community life are of the greatest importance to her, as expressed in 'The sun is there', written at a time when she feared that the youngest of her seven children was in danger of dying from a brain haemorrhage; mercifully, he lived.

Ivor Gurney (1890-1937) was known during his lifetime as a composer, but since his death he has been recognised as one of the major poets of the First World War. After being wounded and gassed in the trenches he became mentally unstable, suffering hallucinations and tormented by 'tricks of electricity', spending the rest of his life in an insane asylum where he nevertheless wrote some of his most powerful poems.

OSCAR HAMMERSTEIN II (1895-1960) was an American lyricist and producer of musical theatre, whose most successful partnership was with Richard Rogers in musicals such as *The Sound of Music* and *Carousel,* in which 'You'll Never Walk Alone' appeared. The song was a number one hit in the UK for Gerry and the Pacemakers in 1963, after which it was adopted by fans at Liverpool Football Club and has been an anthem on the terraces ever since.

MINNIE LOUISE HASKINS (1875-1957) was a lecturer in sociology at the London School of Economics, described by a colleague as 'a woman of unusual capacity and character, with a rare understanding and sympathy... combined with a great deal of love and interest in people'. 'The Gate of the Year' was quoted by King George VI in his Christmas Day Broadcast in 1939, when Britain stood alone against Nazi Germany in the early months of the Second World War.

W E HENLEY (1849-1903) suffered from tubercular arthritis from the age of twelve, which led to the amputation of his left leg and kept him in hospital for long periods. Some of his most powerful writing appears in the twenty-six poems of *In Hospital,* which graphically recount his experiences there. His vigorous and combative personality gave his friend Robert Louis Stevenson the idea for the character of the one-legged Long John Silver in *Treasure Island* (1883).

GEORGE HERBERT (1593-1633) was one of the greatest of English devotional poets. After a distinguished career at Cambridge University and as MP for Montgomeryshire, he became vicar of Bemerton, near Salisbury, where he was greatly loved for his humility and charity to the lowliest of his parishioners. His poetry, though complex and subtle in form, was written in plain, informal language as a conversation, he said, 'between God and my Soul'.

MOLLY HOLDEN (1927-81) was born in Peckham, south London, and later lived in Swindon, where the ancient features of the Wiltshire landscape caught her imagination and provided powerful inspiration for her poetry. When she was thirty-three her poetic focus turned to the effect on her of the illness that eventually killed her – multiple sclerosis – the progress of which she wrote about with great sensitivity and imagination.

HENRY SCOTT HOLLAND (1847-1918), a canon of St Paul's Cathedral, London, was keenly concerned about social justice and was a founder of the Christian Social Union in 1889, advocating the 'Christianisation of the social structure whereby all men live in accordance with the principles of divine justice and human brotherhood'. 'Death is nothing at all' is a verse rendering of part of a sermon he gave at the funeral service for King Edward VII in 1910.

THOMAS HOOD (1799-1845) was a poet, humorist and journalist, known mainly for his fantastical comic verse about politics and public affairs but also for his invective against sweated labour, 'The Song of the Shirt'. When he succumbed to tuberculosis and his family suffered extreme hardship, his Fleet Street friends applied to the Prime Minister, Sir Robert Peel, for financial assistance, and Hood thus became one of the first literary recipients of an award from the 'Civil List'.

GERARD MANLEY HOPKINS (1844-89) was a poet, academic and Jesuit priest. His poetry was highly idiosyncratic and experimental, marked especially by his ecstatic response to the natural world in which he saw the living presence of his Saviour. His fondness for alliteration, internal rhyme and word-clusters, deriving from medieval and native Welsh verse, prefigured and influenced many poets of later periods.

CATIE JENKINS (b1978; now Cate Allison) was born in Beverley, East Yorkshire, and contracted ME at the age of twenty while she was at university. 'Please Don't' was one of several writings that helped her release the creativity she felt was trapped by her long illness. She has now recovered enough to be able to work helping disabled students at Hull University, and is returning to a full-time degree course this year.

ELIZABETH JENNINGS (1926-2001) was unusual in devoting almost all her working life exclusively to poetry. Her writing is distinguished by the visionary intensity and meditative poise of her concern with the spiritual dimensions of experience – of her Roman Catholic faith, her love of art and of Italy, the value she placed in deep friendship, and the nervous breakdown she suffered in mid-life. 'Pain' is one of eight poems in her Sequence in Hospital.

JOHN KEATS (1795-1821), the youngest of the great Romantic poets, died of tuberculosis after only four years of high achievement as a poet. His principal works are the three famous Odes ('To Autumn', 'On a Grecian Urn' and 'To a Nightingale'), 'La Belle Dame Sans Merci', and 'The Eve of St Agnes'. He died after travelling to Rome in the hope of improving his health, where his grave is to be found with its unforgettable inscription: 'Here lies one whose name was writ in water'.

JANE KENYON (1947-95) was born in Ann Arbor, Michigan, where she went to university and met the older poet Donald Hall, with whom she moved to his family farm in New Hampshire. She became the state's Poet Laureate, publishing several volumes of spare, introspective verse, some of it reflecting the depression and other illnesses she suffered from for much of her life. She died of leukemia.

RUDYARD KIPLING (1865-1936), the unofficial 'Poet Laureate of the British Empire', was also a short-story writer and novelist chiefly remembered for his celebrations of imperial Britain in short stories, poems about British soldiers in India, and tales for children. His best-known writings are the children's stories *The Jungle Books*, *The Just So Stories* and *Puck of Pook's Hill*, and the poem most frequently cited as Britain's favourite, 'If'.

JAMES KIRKUP (1918-2009) was a prolific poet, translator and travel writer. He lived for much of his adult life in Japan, where he was professor of English at various universities. His sophisticated, elegant poetry covers a broad range of subjects, especially Japanese culture, but his interest in homoerotic themes brought him notoriety in 1977 when he was prosecuted for blasphemy for writing a poem, soon regretted, about the crucified Christ.

PÄR LAGERKVIST (1891-1974) was a Swedish poet, playwright and novelist, whose central theme was the search for good in a world of evil. His most famous work is his novel *Barabbas* (1950), in which the thief and murderer Barabbas, released by Pontius Pilate in preference to Jesus Christ, spends the rest of his life trying to come to terms with the freedom he gained at the expense of the Messiah. In 1951 Lagerkvist was awarded the Nobel Prize for Literature.

PHILIP LARKIN (1922-85), considered by many the finest British poet of the second half of the twentieth century, lived an uneventful life as librarian at Hull University. Though he is often thought of as gloomy, anti-romantic and xenophobic, his poetry is widely admired for its grace, its understated, colloquial manner, its wit, and its deep understanding of shared human values.

D H LAWRENCE (1885-1930) is most famous as the author of *Lady Chatterley's Lover* and other novels describing love and sexual relationships between men and women, yet he also wrote almost 800 poems that are equally untrammelled, original, and colourfully expressed, powerfully conveying the intensity of feeling he experienced. 'Shadows' was written when he was dying of the tuberculosis he had suffered from for most of his adult life.

DAVID LEES (b 1954) was born in Stoke-on-Trent and taught science and physics in comprehensive schools in Bristol and London until 1995, when he developed ME and had to retire. He is still quite severely affected by the disease, and has published several poems and articles about his experience of illness.

GWYNETH LEWIS (b 1959) was the first National Poet of Wales (2005-2006). After a distinguished academic career in Cambridge, she worked first as a journalist in New York, then became a documentary producer and director at BBC Wales, but gave that up to sail around the world researching ports linked historically with inhabitants of her native city, Cardiff. She has written about her experience of depression both in poetry and in her study *Sunbathing in the Rain: A Cheerful Book on Depression.*

HENRY LONGFELLOW (1807-82), author of *The Song of Hiawatha,* 'Paul Revere's Ride' and 'The Golden Legend', was the first American poet to achieve world-wide fame, and after his death he received from Queen Victoria the unique honour, for an American at that time, of being commemorated in Poets' Corner in Westminster Abbey. After his death, however, he was written off as ridiculously Victorian, and only recently has his true genius been rediscovered.

MARY MCCARTHY lives and writes in Berkeley, California, and has been published in many regional publications. She has been a teacher and a social worker, and is now in active retirement. Flannery O'Connor, author of the epigraph to 'Lupus', was an American Catholic novelist, author of *Wise Blood,* and a well-known sufferer from the disease. (*Lupus* is Latin for wolf.)

HUGH MACDIARMID (1892-1978), born Christopher Murray Grieve, was a leading light in the twentieth-century Scottish Renaissance and a founder member of the National Party of Scotland (precursor of the Scottish National Party). For a time he wrote purely in Scots in order to try to revive the use of the language in Scottish public life, writing his most famous book, *A Drunk Man Looks at a Thistle,* in the language.

ANNA MCKENZIE: attempts by the editor to make contact with this poet have been unsuccessful. Her poem 'Starting Over' appeared in Sheila Cassidy's *Good Friday People* (1991).

JOHN G MAGEE (1922-41) was the son of missionaries, one English and one American, and was brought up in the Far East, England, America and Canada. During the Second World War he served as a test pilot in the RAF, and it was after test-flying a new Spitfire model at high altitude that he wrote his sonnet 'High Flight'. He was killed a few months later in a mid-air collision with a trainee pilot.

GERDA MAYER (*b*1927) was born in Karlsbad, Czechoslovakia, and at the outbreak of the Second World War, in 1939, came to England with one of the *Kindertransport* evacuations of Jewish children from Nazi Germany. After leaving school she worked on the land and then as a secretary in London. She married and remained in England, publishing several books of verse, many of her poems being widely anthologised.

MARY MESTECKY (*b* 1938) was born in Aberystwyth and has been teaching English and drama all her life, first as a graduate assistant in the USA, then in England in schools, university adult education, a young offenders' institution, and English in Language Schools. She has had many poems and children's stories published, and was a finalist in a national poetry speaking competition.

SASHA MOORSOM (1931-93) was one of the BBC's first women producers and was also a writer, painter, sculptor, photographer and poet. She was a prodigious organiser of events and institutions such as the Open College of the Arts (now part of the Open University) and the Lauderdale House arts centre in Highgate. She wrote ' The Company of the Birds' shortly before she died of cancer.

EDITH NESBIT (1858-1924), 'the first modern writer for children', was the author of over sixty children's books, among them

The Railway Children, which broke with tradition by being realistic and challenging instead of make-believe and divorced from children's lives. She was also a political activist and co-founder of the Fabian Society, precursor of the Labour Party.

JOHN O'DONOHUE (1956-2008), for some years a Catholic priest, was an Irish poet and philosopher whose visionary writings and poetry popularised a new spirituality derived from ancient Celtic wisdom. He died in his sleep at the age of fifty-four. The quoted verse is from his *Benedictus: A Book of Blessings*: 'A blessing is a circle of light drawn around a person to protect, heal and strengthen.'

FATHER WILLIAM J O'MALLEY (*b*1928) is an American Jesuit priest, author and actor. He taught theology and English at schools in New York, and has also directed countless theatre productions with students and their parents. He is widely known for playing the role of Fr Dyer in the horror film *The Exorcist* (1973). He has written over thirty spiritual books, including *Daily Prayers for Busy People* and a sequel, in which the quoted verses appear.

MARY OLIVER (*b* 1935) is a natural successor to Walt Whitman, the originator of lyrical free verse in America, and Henry Thoreau, the poet-naturalist who anticipated the concerns of the modern ecology movement. She has been called 'an indefatigable guide to the natural world', and her poetry reveals parables and revelations of the human condition, making her one of America's best-loved poets.

COVENTRY PATMORE (1823-96) was a major but now almost forgotten Victorian poet, best known for his long poem about an ideal happy marriage, *The Angel in the House*. (He married three times, losing his first two wives to early death.) The themes of much of his later verse were love, death, grief, and immortality. He worked as a librarian at the British Museum, and was an important literary member of the Pre-Raphaelite Brotherhood.

ST PAUL (*c* 5-*c* 57) was a Roman Jew whose miraculous conversion to Christianity on the road to Damascus led him to cease persecuting the followers of Jesus to become the most influential of the early Christian missionaries. In his extensive letters to fellow Christians in the Mediterranean world, he expounded the teachings of Jesus and explained how the faith should direct the Christian in the conduct of daily life.

RUTH PITTER (1897-1992) worked for most of her life producing decorative painted furniture and trays, but she was also well known as a poet and for her appearances as a guest on radio programmes and on the television discussion programme *The Brains Trust*. She was highly praised for her poetry by W B Yeats, C S Lewis and Thom Gunn, and was the first woman to receive the Queen's Gold Medal for Poetry.

PO CHU-Ï (772-846) – 'Bai Ju-yi' in pinyin (Chinese) – was an official in the service of the Emperor of China and a revered poet both in his lifetime and to this day. When he was in his thirties he succumbed to a mysterious debilitating illness which lasted for at least four years, during which time he practised Buddhist meditation, which no doubt aided his full recovery.

KATHLEEN RAINE (1908-2003) was a spiritual poet in the tradition of W B Yeats and William Blake, about whom she wrote extensively.

She believed in the sacred nature of all life, and the power of poetry to express and preserve essential truths. She held a chair at Cambridge University and also taught at Harvard and elsewhere. In 1990 she founded a 'new school of wisdom', the Temenos Academy for Education in the Light of the Spirit.

RAINER MARIA RILKE (1875-1926), born in Prague, Bohemia (now the Czech Republic), is one of the most influential poets in the German language and, in translation, in Europe and America. A constant theme in his poetry is the coexistence of two realms, the spiritual and the material, and the role of creativity in bridging the two. He died of leukemia in a Swiss sanatorium.

A MARY F ROBINSON (1857-1944) was an English poet, novelist, and reviewer of French literature. Having lived for much of her life in France, where she co-founded the prestigious literary award the Prix Femina, she is better remembered there than in her native country, where she is almost forgotten.

E A ROBINSON (1869-1935) was an American poet who pursued a life of poverty for the sake of his poetry. By chance, however, a volume of his verse came into the hands of President Theodore Roosevelt, who publicly lauded the poet and arranged a sinecure for him so that he could continue writing. His poetry excels in portraying responses to adversity in ordinary people who fail on a material level but succeed on the moral or spiritual plane.

THEODORE ROETHKE (1908-63) – pronounced 'RETkee' – was an American poet and son of an owner of commercial greenhouses, an environment that inspired his love of nature and was the subject of some of his finest poems. He taught English Literature and Creative Writing at various universities, though his career was interrupted by bouts of severe mental illness which he wrote about in several poems, viewing them as spiritual crises relating to God and Eternity.

CHRISTINA ROSSETTI (1830-94) was the sister of and model for the Pre-Raphaelite painter and poet Dante Gabriel Rossetti and a considerable author in her own right of devotional, romantic and children's verse. At the age of fourteen she suffered a nervous breakdown, followed by periods of depression for much of her life. Her best-known poems are 'Remember', 'Goblin Market', and the Christmas hymns 'In the bleak midwinter' and 'Love came down at Christmas'.

SIEGFRIED SASSOON (1886-1967) was one of the best-known poets and critics of the First World War, when as an officer he was famed for his reckless exploits at the Front. Before joining up he had lived a privileged life of hunting, playing golf and writing verse which he published privately. After the war he wrote his celebrated *Memoirs of a Foxhunting Man* about his pre-war life, and *Memoirs of an Infantry Officer* about his wartime experiences.

CAROLE SATYAMURTI (*b* 1939), a poet and sociologist, grew up in Kent and has lived in the United States, Singapore and Uganda. For many years she taught at the University of East London and at the Tavistock Clinic. She also has long experience as a poetry and creative writing workshop tutor. Among her many books is a collection of essays on the connections between poetry and psychoanalysis, *Acquainted with the Night: Psychoanalysis and the Poetic Imagination*.

VERNON SCANNELL (1922-2007) was a prolific poet and novelist, who set some of his novels in the world of boxing, in which he had fought at a professional level. He had also been a soldier, a deserter for two years, and a teacher, and his varied experiences provided material for several adventurous autobiographies. His poetry reflects his fascination with risk-taking but also his compassionate interest in ordinary human life.

WILLIAM SHAKESPEARE (1564-1616) is regarded the world over as the greatest of all English poets and dramatists, and revered for his humanity, versatility and unequalled poetic power. Besides his thirty-eight plays, his poetry consists mainly of the 154 sonnets on love, beauty, and mortality. Of his personal life he left little trace, but was remembered by contemporaries as 'a good-natured Man, of great sweetness in his Manners, and a most agreeable Companion'.

WILLIAM SOUTAR (1898-1943) was a leading poet of the twentieth-century Scottish Renaissance. When he was twenty-six he was diagnosed with ankylosing spondylitis, an inflammation of the spine, which confined him to bed and from which he died twenty years later. He is best remembered for his vernacular Scots lyrics and his *Diaries of a Dying Man*.

MARIA LUISA SPAZIANI (*b* 1924) is an Italian poet, translator, scholar and journalist. She was deeply influenced by the modernist lyric poet Eugenio Montale, and after his death helped found the Universitas Montaliana and Italy's most prestigious poetry prize, the Premio Montale. She taught German and French literature at the University of Messina in Sicily for twenty-five years, and has been nominated three times for the Nobel Prize for Literature.

Rabindranath Tagore (1861-1941) was an Indian Bengali mystic poet, philosopher and musician, the most highly regarded writer in Indian literature. His reputation in the West rests on his approximately 1000 poems, in particular the *Gitanjali*, 103 short poems on the love of God. In 1913 he became the first Indian to receive the Nobel Prize for Literature.

Alison Tavendale (*b*1948) was born in London and has been writing all her life – poetry, stories, and radio plays. She has worked as a hospital and hospice social worker and now runs therapeutic writing workshops. She lives in Aberdeenshire and cares for hurt or abandoned animals: 'It is the best feeling in the world, to see a wild creature I have helped, walk or fly away'. She has lived with ME since 2003.

Alfred, Tennyson (1809-92) was widely venerated in his lifetime by his fellow countrymen and is still one of the most popular poets in the English language. His best-known poems are 'The Lady of Shalott', 'The Charge of the Light Brigade', and *In Memoriam*, a series of 133 meditations on his search for hope after the death of his friend Arthur Hallam. He was the longest-serving Poet Laureate in the history of the post, having held it for forty-one years.

Dylan Thomas (1914-53) was the most characteristically Welsh of modern Welsh poets, and 'Fern Hill' is one of his best-known poems. Describing childhood holidays on a Welsh farm, it is a typical example of his rhapsodic style, heavily influenced by G M Hopkins's alliteration and mystical exuberance, combined with Biblical cadences derived from the Chapel services Thomas heard as a child. The radio play *Under Milk Wood* is a fantasy based on the small fishing village where he lived.

R S Thomas (1913-2000) was a poet and priest in the Church of Wales, serving in small parishes which form the background of much of his characteristically bleak yet compassionate poetry. He had an intense love of Wales, though he felt that its troubled history, downtrodden as it was by the English, had left its people culturally impoverished. His poems meditating on the nature of God are always filled with hope, but rarely offer consolation or resolution.

Chidiock Tichborne (c 1558-86) came from an ardently Catholic landed family during a time of dangerous conflict between the Roman Catholic and Protestant faiths. When Queen Elizabeth I outlawed the Roman faith, Tichborne became involved in a conspiracy to assassinate her and restore Rome's supremacy in England. The plot was discovered, and Tichborne was hung, drawn and quartered, an execution involving live disembowelling.

Tomas Tranströmer (b1931) is regarded as Sweden's best poet since the Second World War, though his main occupation has been as a psychologist working in juvenile prisons as well as with drug addicts and the disabled. His poetic style is characterised by a visionary sense of reality expressed in precise images, often contrasting spiritual with mental awareness and making unexpected connections between the two.

Derek Walcott (b 1930) was born in the Caribbean island of St Lucia and has lived for most of his life in Trinidad and the United States, where he has held several university posts. He is a poet, playwright and painter whose work is dominated by the theme of myth and its relation to culture. His best-known work is the epic poem *Omeros*, a reworking of Homer's dramas in a Caribbean setting. He was awarded the Nobel Prize for Literature in 1992.

WALT WHITMAN (1819-92), perhaps the most loved of American poets, had little education and trained as a printer, a trade that enabled him to print his own poetry at will. At an early age he fell in love with the Bible, echoes of which can be found throughout his free-ranging, unconventional verse of which his masterpiece is *Leaves of Grass*, a paean in verse to the whole of human life and the dignity of Man.

ELLA WHEELER WILCOX (1850-1919) was an American journalist, novelist, and a highly prolific poet who often wrote two or more poems a day. She was the most popular American poet of the nineteenth century, though after her death she was mercilessly parodied then largely forgotten except for the opening two lines of the quoted verse, though these are not really her own, being a paraphrase of lines by Shakespeare.

JAN WILLIAMS (*b* 1953) grew up on a farm in Herefordshire, raised a family, and pursued an academic career in health promotion. At the age of forty-three she fell ill with ME, and during the ten years that followed wrote poetry to try to make sense of her experience of sickness and loss. She now teaches others the same mind–body skills that she used to recover her own health.

W B YEATS (1865-1939) was an Irish poet, dramatist and politician, leader of the Irish Literary Revival and one of the most important figures in twentieth-century poetry. He had a lifelong interest in mysticism, the esoteric, and in Irish folk tales, which he saw as an important part of Ireland's national heritage and a means of reviving its Celtic identity. He was awarded the Nobel Prize for Literature in 1922.

INDEX OF POETS, TITLES AND FIRST LINES